180 Best-Ever Recipes For
VEGETARIANS

180 Best-Ever Recipes For
VEGETARIANS

Delicious easy-to-make dishes for every occasion, with over 200 tempting photographs

Contributing Editor: Martha Day

southwater

Notes

Bracketed terms are intended for American readers.

For all recipes, quantities are given in both metric and imperial measures and, where appropriate, in standard cups and spoons. Follow one set, but not a mixture, because they are not interchangeable.

Standard spoon and cup measures are level.
1 tsp=5ml, 1 tbsp=15ml, 1 cup=250ml/8fl oz.

Australian standard tablespoons are 20ml. Australian readers should use 3 tsp in place of 1 tbsp for measuring small quantities of gelatine, flour, salt etc.

American pints are 16fl oz/2 cups. American readers should use 20fl oz/½ cups in place of 1 pint when measuring liquids.

Electric oven temperatures in this book are for conventional ovens. When using a fan oven, the temperature will probably need to be reduced by about 10–20°C/20–40°F. Since ovens vary, you should check with your manufacturer's instruction book for guidance.

The nutritional analysis given for each recipe is calculated per portion (i.e. serving or item), unless otherwise stated. If the recipe gives a range, such as Serves 4–6, then the nutritional analysis will be for the smaller portion size, i.e. serves 6.

Medium (US large) eggs are used unless otherwise stated.

This edition is published by Southwater, an imprint of Anness Publishing Ltd, Hermes House, 88–89 Blackfriars Road, London SE1 8HA; tel. 020 7401 2077; fax 020 7633 9499

www.southwaterbooks.com; www.annesspublishing.com

If you like the images in this book and would like to investigate using them for publishing, promotions or advertising, please visit our website www.practicalpictures.com for more information.

UK agent: The Manning Partnership Ltd
   tel. 01225 478444; fax 01225 478440; sales@manning-partnership.co.uk
UK distributor: Grantham Book Services Ltd
   tel. 01476 541080; fax 01476 541061; orders@gbs.tbs-ltd.co.uk
North American agent/distributor: National Book Network
   tel. 301 459 3366; fax 301 429 5746; www.nbnbooks.com
Australian agent/distributor: Pan Macmillan Australia
   tel. 1300 135 113; fax 1300 135 103; customer.service@macmillan.com.au
New Zealand agent/distributor: David Bateman Ltd
   tel. (09) 415 7664; fax (09) 415 8892

Publisher: Joanna Lorenz
Editorial Director: Helen Sudell
Editors: Simona Hill and Elizabeth Woodland
Design: SMI
Cover Design: Nigel Partridge
Photographers: Karl Adamson, Edward Allwright, Steve Baxter, James Duncan, Michelle Garrett, Amanda Heywood, Don Last, Patrick McLeavy, Michael Michaels
Additional photography: Sopexa UK
Recipes: Carla Capalbo, Maxine Clark, Frances Cleary, Carole Clements, Roz Denny, Christine France, Sarah Gates, Shirley Gill, Rosamund Grant, Sue Maggs, Annie Nichols, Jenny Stacey, Liz Trigg, Hilaire Walden, Laura Washburn, Steven Wheeler, Elizabeth Wolf-Cohen
Food for Photography: Joanne Craig, Wendy Lee, Jenny Shapter, Jane Stevenson, Elizabeth Wolf-Cohen
Home Economists: Carla Capalbo, Jenny Shapter
Stylists: Madeleine Brehaut, Carla Capalbo, Michelle Garrett, Hilary Guy, Amanda Heywood, Blake Minton, Kirsty Rawlings, Rebecca Sturrock, Fiona Tillett
Production Controller: Mai-Ling Collyer

Ethical Trading Policy

At Anness Publishing we believe that business should be conducted in an ethical and ecologically sustainable way, with respect for the environment and a proper regard to the replacement of the natural resources we employ.

As a publisher, we use a lot of wood pulp to make high-quality paper for printing, and that wood commonly comes from spruce trees. We are therefore currently growing more than 750,000 trees in three Scottish forest plantations: Berrymoss (130 hectares/320 acres), West Touxhill (125 hectares/305 acres) and Deveron Forest (75 hectares/185 acres). The forests we manage contain more than 3.5 times the number of trees employed each year in making paper for the books we manufacture.

Because of this ongoing ecological investment programme, you, as our customer, can have the pleasure and reassurance of knowing that a tree is being cultivated on your behalf to naturally replace the materials used to make the book you are holding.

Our forestry programme is run in accordance with the UK Woodland Assurance Scheme (UKWAS) and will be certified by the internationally recognized Forest Stewardship Council (FSC). The FSC is a non-government organization dedicated to promoting responsible management of the world's forests. Certification ensures forests are managed in an environmentally sustainable and socially responsible way. For further information about this scheme, go to www.annesspublishing.com/trees.

Cover illustrations

Front cover main image: Fried Tomatoes with Herb Polenta, p43; *bottom row, from left to right:* Thai Noodle Salad p28; Mushroom Flan, p46; Curried Parsnip Soup, p14; Rocket and Tomato Pizza, p66.

Previously published as part of a larger volume, *500 Best-Ever Recipes*.

Contents

Introduction

It is not only vegetarians who can enjoy vegetarian food. The fresh, light and innovative recipes that have come to the forefront of new-style vegetarian cuisine provide a tempting

alternative to some of the heavier, non-vegetarian dishes.

Through vegetarian cooking, you can mix and match the vibrant colours, textures and flavours of vegetables, fruits, pulses and grains with many other exciting ingredients, and experiment with a wide variety of interesting and unusual foods to create all kinds of delicious and tempting dishes from many parts of the world. This book gathers together some of the best-loved vegetarian recipes from around the globe, all of them packed with fabulous tastes and textures.

There are over 180 delicious and easy-to-follow vegetarian recipes for all the family to enjoy. There is a fine selection of hearty soups and appetizers, such as White Bean Soup and Country Vegetable Soup, which are satisfying enough for a light meal yet attractive enough to serve at an impressive dinner party. Sophisticated vegetables and salads include Broccoli Cauliflower Gratin and Ratatouille, Goat's Cheese Salad and Chicory, Fruit and Nut Salad. Flavoursome main courses include Baked Squash with Parmesan and Tomato and Basil Tart, both classic dishes that will tantalize your tastebuds. Also included is a variety of more unusual dishes, such as Spinach and Hazelnut Lasagne and Lentil Stir-fry. The desserts range from a light Apricot Mousse and smooth Brown Bread Ice Cream to a rich Warm Lemon and Syrup Cake.

This collection of recipes has been drawn together from the combined talents of some of the world's most respected cooks and food writers. With the help of this authoritative guide, your cooking will not only withstand the scrutiny of your most demanding critics – be it yourself or a fierce rival – but will win them over in style.

With options for everything from soups and appetizers to special occasion dinners, every recipe here is delicious proof that eating the vegetarian way is not only nutritious, but entertaining and exciting too. Try them and enjoy them.

Leek, Potato & Rocket Soup

Rocket, with its distinctive peppery taste, is wonderful in this filling soup. Serve it hot with ciabatta croûtons.

Serves 4–6
50g/2oz/4 tbsp butter
1 onion, chopped
3 leeks, chopped
2 potatoes, diced

900ml/1½ pints/3¾ cups
  vegetable stock
2 large handfuls rocket (arugula),
  coarsely chopped
150ml/¼ pint/⅔ cup double
  (heavy) cream
salt and ground black pepper
garlic-flavoured ciabatta croûtons,
  to serve

1 Melt the butter in a large heavy pan over low heat. Add the onion, leeks and potatoes and stir until all the vegetable pieces are well coated in butter.

2 Cover with a tight-fitting lid and cook for about 15 minutes, until the vegetables are just beginning to soften but do not let them colour. Pour in the stock, bring to the boil and cover again with the lid, then simmer for a further 20 minutes, until the vegetables are tender.

3 Press the soup through a sieve (strainer) or food mill and return to the rinsed-out pan. (When puréeing the soup, don't use a blender or food processor, as these will give the soup a gluey texture.) Add the chopped rocket, stir in and cook gently for about 5 minutes.

4 Stir in the cream, then season to taste with salt and pepper. Reheat gently but do not boil. Ladle the soup into warmed soup bowls, sprinkle a few ciabatta croûtons into each one and serve immediately.

> **Cook's Tip**
> *To make the croûtons, cut the bread into 1cm/½ in cubes, without the crust if you wish, and either fry or bake in a roasting pan in oil until golden and crunchy.*

Carrot & Coriander Soup

Use a good home-made stock for this soup – it adds a far greater depth of flavour than stock made from cubes or powder. The latter may also have an unhealthily high salt content.

Serves 4
50g/2oz/4 tbsp butter
2 leeks, sliced

450g/1lb carrots, sliced
15ml/1 tbsp ground coriander
1.2 litres/2 pints/5 cups vegetable
  stock
150ml/¼ pint/⅔ cup Greek
  (US strained plain) yogurt
salt and ground black pepper
30–45ml/2–3 tbsp chopped
  fresh coriander (cilantro),
  to garnish

1 Melt the butter in a large pan over low heat. Add the leeks and carrots and stir well, coating the vegetables with the butter. Cover with a tight-fitting lid and cook for about 10 minutes, until the vegetables are just beginning to soften but do not let them colour.

2 Stir in the ground coriander and cook for about 1 minute. Pour in the stock and season to taste with salt and pepper. Bring to the boil, cover and simmer for about 20 minutes, until the leeks and carrots are tender.

3 Leave to cool slightly, then ladle the soup into a blender, in batches if necessary, and process until smooth. Return the soup to the pan and add about 30ml/2 tbsp of the yogurt, then taste the soup and adjust the seasoning again to taste. Reheat gently but do not boil.

4 Ladle the soup into bowls and put a spoonful of the remaining yogurt in the centre of each. Sprinkle with the coriander and serve immediately.

> **Variation**
> *For a non-vegetarian version of this soup, substitute a good-quality chicken stock for the vegetable stock.*

Carrot Energy 195kcal/807kJ; Protein 4.6g; Carbohydrate 12.3g, of which sugars 11.1g; Fat 14.9g, of which saturates 8.7g; Cholesterol 27mg; Calcium 108mg; Fibre 4.6g; Sodium 132mg.
Leek Energy 245kcal/1015kJ; Protein 3g; Carbohydrate 11.9g, of which sugars 3.7g; Fat 20.9g, of which saturates 12.8g; Cholesterol 52mg; Calcium 54mg; Fibre 2.7g; Sodium 75mg.

Tomato & Basil Soup

In the summer, when tomatoes are both plentiful and inexpensive, this is a lovely soup to make.

Serves 4
30ml/2 tbsp olive oil
I onion, chopped
2.5ml/½ tsp caster
  (superfine) sugar
I carrot, finely chopped
I potato, finely chopped
I garlic clove, crushed
675g/1½lb ripe tomatoes,
  coarsely chopped
5ml/I tsp tomato purée (paste)
I bay leaf
I thyme sprig
I oregano sprig
4 fresh basil leaves, coarsely torn
300ml/½ pint/1¼ cups vegetable
  stock
2–3 pieces sun-dried tomatoes in
  oil, drained
30ml/2 tbsp shredded fresh
  basil leaves
salt and ground black pepper

1 Heat the oil in a large pan over low heat. Add the onion, sprinkle with the sugar and cook gently for 5 minutes.

2 Add the chopped carrot and potato, stir well, then cover the pan with a tight-fitting lid and cook gently for a further 10 minutes, until the vegetables are beginning to soften but do not let them colour.

3 Stir in the garlic, tomatoes, tomato purée, bay leaf, thyme, oregano, torn basil leaves and stock and season to taste with salt and pepper. Cover the pan again with the lid and simmer gently for 25–30 minutes, or until the vegetables are tender.

4 Remove the pan from the heat and press the soup through a sieve (strainer) or food mill to extract all the skins and seeds. Taste the soup and season again with salt and pepper.

5 Return the soup to the rinsed-out pan and reheat gently, then ladle into four warmed soup bowls. Finely chop the sun-dried tomatoes and mix with a little of the oil from the jar. Add a spoonful to each serving, then sprinkle the shredded basil over the top and serve immediately.

White Bean Soup

Small white lima beans or pinto beans work well in this soup, or try butter beans for a change.

Serves 6
350g/12oz/1½ cups dried
  cannellini or other white beans
I bay leaf
75ml/5 tbsp olive oil
I onion, finely chopped
I carrot, finely chopped
I celery stick, finely chopped
3 tomatoes, peeled and
  finely chopped
2 garlic cloves, finely chopped
5ml/I tsp fresh thyme leaves or
  2.5ml/½ tsp dried thyme
750ml/1¼ pints/3 cups boiling
  water
salt and ground black pepper
extra virgin olive oil, to serve

1 Pick over the beans carefully, discarding any stones or other particles. Place the beans in a large bowl, add cold water to cover and leave to soak overnight. Drain well.

2 Place the beans in a large pan, add water to cover, bring to the boil and cook for 20 minutes. Drain, return the beans to the pan, cover with cold water and bring to the boil again. Add the bay leaf and cook 1–2 hours, until the beans are tender. Drain again. Remove and discard the bay leaf.

3 Spoon about three-quarters of the beans into a food processor or blender and process to a purée. Alternatively, pass through a food mill, adding a little water if necessary.

4 Heat the oil in a large pan over medium heat. Add the onion and cook, stirring occasionally, for about 5 minutes, until softened but not coloured. Add the carrot and celery and cook, stirring occasionally, for a further 5 minutes.

5 Stir in the tomatoes, garlic and fresh or dried thyme. Cook, stirring frequently, for 6–8 minutes more.

6 Pour in the boiling water. Stir in the beans and the bean purée and season to taste with salt and pepper. Simmer for 10–15 minutes. Ladle into warmed soup bowls, drizzle with a little extra virgin olive oil and serve immediately.

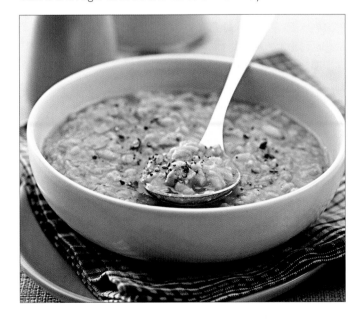

Tomato Energy 129kcal/538kJ; Protein 2.2g; Carbohydrate 13.4g, of which sugars 9.2g; Fat 7.8g, of which saturates 1.3g; Cholesterol 0mg; Calcium 26mg; Fibre 3g; Sodium 30mg.
Bean Energy 249kcal/1050kJ; Protein 13.3g; Carbohydrate 28g, of which sugars 3.7g; Fat 10.2g, of which saturates 1.5g; Cholesterol 0mg; Calcium 66mg; Fibre 9.9g; Sodium 20mg.

Spiced Parsnip Soup

This pale, creamy-textured soup is given a special touch with an aromatic garlic and mustard seed garnish.

Serves 4–6

40g/1½oz/3 tbsp butter
1 onion, chopped
675g/1½lb parsnips, diced
5ml/1 tsp ground coriander
2.5ml/½ tsp ground cumin
2.5ml/½ tsp ground turmeric
1.5ml/¼ tsp chilli powder
1.2 litres/2 pints/5 cups vegetable stock
150ml/¼ pint/⅔ cup single (light) cream
15ml/1 tbsp sunflower oil
1 garlic clove, cut into julienne strips
10ml/2 tsp yellow mustard seeds
salt and ground black pepper

1 Melt the butter in a large pan over medium heat. Add the onion and parsnips and cook gently, stirring occasionally, for about 3 minutes.

2 Stir in the spices and cook for 1 minute more. Add the stock, season to taste with salt and pepper and bring to the boil, then reduce the heat. Cover with a tight-fitting lid and simmer for about 45 minutes, until the parsnips are tender.

3 Cool slightly, then ladle the soup into a blender and process until smooth. Return the soup to the rinsed-out pan, add the cream and heat through gently over low heat.

4 Heat the oil in a small pan, add the julienne strips of garlic and yellow mustard seeds and cook briskly, stirring occasionally, until the garlic is beginning to brown and the mustard seeds start to pop and splutter. Remove the pan from the heat.

5 Ladle the soup into warmed soup bowls and pour a little of the hot spice mixture over each. Serve immediately.

Variation
Crushed coriander seeds may be substituted for the mustard seeds in the garnish.

Pumpkin Soup

The flavour of this soup will develop and improve if it is made a day in advance.

Serves 4–6

900g/2lb pumpkin
45ml/3 tbsp olive oil
2 onions, chopped
2 celery sticks, chopped
450g/1lb tomatoes, chopped
1.5 litres/2½ pints/6¼ cups vegetable stock
30ml/2 tbsp tomato purée (paste)
1 bouquet garni
creme friâche
30ml/2 tbsp chopped fresh flat leaf parsley
salt and ground black pepper

1 With a sharp knife cut the pumpkin into thin slices, discarding the skin and seeds.

2 Heat the olive oil in a large pan over medium heat. Add the onions and celery and cook, stirring occasionally, for about 5 minutes, until the vegetables are beginning to soften but do not let them colour

3 Add the pumpkin slices and tomatoes and cook, stirring occasionally, for a further 5 minutes.

4 Add the vegetable stock, tomato purée and bouquet garni to the pan and season with salt and pepper. Bring the soup to the boil, then reduce the heat to low, cover with a tight-fitting lid and simmer gently for 45 minutes.

5 Leave the soup to cool slightly, then remove and discard the bouquet garni. Ladle the soup into a food processor or blender, in batches if necessary, and process until smooth.

6 Press the soup through a sieve (strainer) and return it to the rinsed-out pan. Reheat gently, then taste and season again if necessary. Ladle the soup into warmed soup bowls. Serve with a spoonful of creme friâche, and sprinkle each serving with the chopped parsley and serve immediately.

Parsnip Energy 187kcal/780kJ; Protein 3g; Carbohydrate 14.8g, of which sugars 7g; Fat 13.3g, of which saturates 7g; Cholesterol 28mg; Calcium 70mg; Fibre 5.2g; Sodium 59mg.
Pumpkin Energy 136kcal/565kJ; Protein 4.6g; Carbohydrate 7.2g, of which sugars 6.2g; Fat 10g, of which saturates 2.4g; Cholesterol 11mg; Calcium 58mg; Fibre 2.6g; Sodium 235mg.

Jerusalem Artichoke Soup

Topped with saffron cream, this unusual soup is wonderful to serve on a chilly winter's day.

Serves 4
50g/2oz/4 tbsp butter
1 onion, chopped
450g/1lb Jerusalem artichokes, peeled and cut into chunks

900ml/1½ pints/3¾ cups vegetable stock
150ml/¼ pint/⅔ cup milk
150ml/¼ pint/⅔ cup double (heavy) cream
large pinch of saffron powder
salt and ground black pepper
chopped fresh chives, to garnish

1 Melt the butter in a large heavy pan over medium heat. Add the onion and cook, stirring occasionally, for 5–8 minutes, until softened but not browned.

2 Add the artichokes to the pan and stir until coated in the butter. Reduce the heat to low, cover the pan with a tight-fitting lid and cook gently for 10–15 minutes but do not let the artichokes brown. Pour in the stock and milk, then cover the pan again and simmer gently for about 15 minutes. Leave the soup to cool slightly, then ladle it into a food processor or blender, in batches if necessary, and process until smooth.

3 Strain the soup back into the rinsed-out pan. Add half the cream, season to taste with salt and pepper and reheat gently.

4 Lightly whip the remaining cream and saffron powder. Ladle the soup into warmed soup bowls and put a spoonful of saffron cream in the centre of each. Sprinkle with the chopped chives and serve immediately.

> **Cook's Tip**
> The flesh of Jerusalem artichokes discolours when it is exposed to the air. Fill a bowl with cold water and add about 30ml/ 2 tbsp lemon juice. As you peel the artichokes drop them into the acidulated water to prevent them from turning brown.

Broccoli & Stilton Soup

A really easy, but deliciously rich, soup – choose something simple and light for the main course, such as Vegetable and Tofu Kebabs.

Serves 4
350g/12oz/3 cups broccoli florets
25g/1oz/2 tbsp butter
1 onion, chopped

1 leek, white part only, chopped
1 small potato, diced
600ml/1 pint/2½ cups hot vegetable stock
300ml/½ pint/1¼ cups milk
45ml/3 tbsp double (heavy) cream
115g/4oz Stilton cheese, rind removed, crumbled
salt and ground black pepper

1 Discard any tough stems from the broccoli florets. Set aside two small florets for the garnish.

2 Melt the butter in a large pan over medium heat. Add the onion and leek and cook, stirring occasionally, for 5–8 minutes, until softened but not coloured.

3 Add the broccoli and potato and pour in the stock. Cover the pan with a tight-fitting lid, reduce the heat to low and simmer for 15–20 minutes, until the vegetables are tender.

4 Leave the soup to cool slightly, then ladle it into a food processor or blender and process until smooth. Strain through a sieve (strainer) back into the rinsed-out pan.

5 Add the milk and cream, season to taste with salt and pepper and reheat gently. When the soup is hot stir in the cheese until it just melts, then remove the pan from the heat. Do not let it come to the boil.

6 Meanwhile, blanch the reserved broccoli florets in lightly salted, boiling water for 1–2 minutes, then drain and cut them vertically into thin slices.

7 Ladle the soup into warmed soup bowls and garnish each with the sliced broccoli florets and a generous grinding of black pepper. Serve immediately.

Artichoke Energy 310kcal/1277kJ; Protein 2.7g; Carbohydrate 4.7g, of which sugars 4.3g; Fat 31.3g, of which saturates 19.4g; Cholesterol 80mg; Calcium 116mg; Fibre 1.5g; Sodium 168mg.
Broccoli Energy 312kcal/1296kJ; Protein 14.4g; Carbohydrate 11.3g, of which sugars 6.8g; Fat 23.3g, of which saturates 14.7g; Cholesterol 60mg; Calcium 251mg; Fibre 3.3g; Sodium 310mg.

Mediterranean Tomato Soup

Children will love this soup – especially if you use fancy pasta such as alphabet or animal shapes.

Serves 4
675g/1½lb ripe plum tomatoes
1 onion, quartered
1 celery stick
1 garlic clove
15ml/1 tbsp olive oil
450ml/¾ pint/scant 2 cups vegetable stock
15ml/2 tbsp tomato purée (paste)
50g/2oz/½ cup small pasta shapes
salt and ground black pepper
fresh coriander (cilantro) or parsley sprigs, to garnish

1 Place the tomatoes, onion, celery and garlic in a pan with the olive oil. Cover with a tight-fitting lid and cook over low heat, shaking the pan occasionally, for 40–45 minutes, until the vegetables become very soft.

2 Leave to cool slightly, then spoon the vegetables into a food processor or blender and process until smooth. Press through a sieve (strainer) to remove the tomato seeds and skins, then return to the rinsed-out pan.

3 Stir in the stock and tomato purée and bring to the boil. Add the pasta and simmer gently for about 8 minutes, or until the pasta is tender. Season with salt and pepper to taste.

4 Ladle the soup into warmed soup bowls, sprinkle with coriander or parsley to garnish and serve immediately.

> **Cook's Tip**
> Plum tomatoes are best for this soup as they have a rich flavour and are less watery than some other varieties. They also have fewer seeds. However other types of tomato can be used, especially if they have been sun-ripened on the vine, which produces a delicious sweetness. Tomatoes that have ripened after picking are really not suitable but if you have to use them, add a good pinch of sugar at the beginning of step 3.

Egg & Lemon Soup with Pasta

This light, nourishing soup, made with egg and lemon, has traditionally been a favourite throughout the Mediterranean. This Greek version contains orzo, tiny rice-shaped pasta, but you can use any small shape of pasta. Serve the soup with thin slices of lightly toasted bread and add a garnish of very thin lemon slices.

Serves 4–6
1.75 litres/3 pints/7½ cups vegetable stock
115g/4oz/½ cup orzo pasta
3 eggs
juice of 1 large lemon
salt and ground black pepper

1 Pour the vegetable stock into a large pan and bring to the boil. Add the orzo pasta or other small pasta shapes and cook for 5 minutes, or according to the packet instructions.

2 Beat the eggs until they are frothy, then add the lemon juice and a tablespoon of cold water. Slowly stir in a ladleful of the hot vegetable stock, then add one or two more.

3 Remove the pan from the heat, then pour in the egg mixture and stir well. Season to taste with salt and freshly ground black pepper and serve immediately.

> **Cook's Tip**
> Do not let the soup boil once the egg and lemon juice mixture has been added, or it will curdle. Take care when using a pan that retains heat because the soup may continue to simmer after the heat has been reduced.

> **Variation**
> Substitute orzo with other small pasta, such as stellette (stars) or orecchiette (little ears). The cooking time should be the same.

Tomato Energy 105kcal/444kJ; Protein 3.1g; Carbohydrate 16.3g, of which sugars 7.1g; Fat 3.5g, of which saturates 0.6g; Cholesterol 0mg; Calcium 23mg; Fibre 2.5g; Sodium 30mg.
Egg and Lemon Energy 107kcal/451kJ; Protein 5.7g; Carbohydrate 14.5g, of which sugars 0.8g; Fat 3.4g, of which saturates 0.8g; Cholesterol 95mg; Calcium 22mg; Fibre 0.6g; Sodium 307mg.

Beetroot & Apricot Swirl

This soup is most attractive if you swirl together the two coloured purées, but mix them together if you prefer.

Serves 4
4 large cooked beetroot (beets), coarsely chopped
1 small onion, coarsely chopped
600ml/1 pint/2½ cups vegetable stock
200g/7oz ready-to-eat dried apricots
250ml/8fl oz/1 cup orange juice
salt and ground black pepper

1 Place the beetroot and half of the onion in a pan with the stock. Bring to the boil, then reduce the heat, cover with a tight-fitting lid and simmer for about 10 minutes. Leave to cool slightly, then ladle the mixture into a food processor or blender, in batches if necessary, and process until smooth. Return to the rinsed-out pan and set aside.

2 Place the remaining onion in another pan with the apricots and orange juice, cover and simmer gently over low heat for about 15 minutes, until tender. Leave to cool slightly, then ladle the mixture into a food processor or blender and process until smooth. Return to the rinsed-out pan.

3 Gently reheat both purées. Season to taste with salt and pepper, then swirl the mixtures together in warmed individual soup bowls to create a marbled effect. Serve immediately.

> **Cook's Tip**
> Beetroot (beets) are widely available ready cooked. To cook your own, first rinse them well under cold running water and trim the stalks to about 2.5cm/1in above the beetroot. Do not peel or cut off the long roots as this will cause the colour to bleed away. Place the beetroot in a pan, add enough water to cover and bring to the boil. Lower the heat, cover and simmer for about 1 hour, until tender. Drain, then peel the beetroot with your fingers when cool enough to handle.

Pasta & Chickpea Soup

The addition of a fresh rosemary sprig creates a typically Mediterranean flavour in this soup.

Serves 4–6
200g/7oz/generous 1 cup dried chickpeas
3 garlic cloves, peeled
1 bay leaf
90ml/6 tbsp olive oil
50g/2oz/¼ cup sun-dried tomatoes, chopped
1 fresh rosemary sprig
600ml/1 pint/2½ cups water
150g/5oz/1¼ cups ditalini or other short hollow pasta
salt and ground black pepper
freshly grated Parmesan cheese, to serve (optional)

1 Place the chickpeas in a bowl, add cold water to cover and leave to soak overnight. Drain, rinse well and drain again.

2 Place the chickpeas in a large pan, add water to cover and bring to the boil. Cook for 15 minutes, then drain, rinse and drain again. Return the chickpeas to the pan. Add water to cover, one garlic clove, the bay leaf, half the olive oil and a pinch of pepper. Bring to the boil, then lower the heat and simmer for about 2 hours, until tender. Add more boiling water if necessary to keep the chickpeas covered.

3 Remove and discard the bay leaf. Pass about half the chickpeas through a food mill or process in a food processor with a little cooking liquid. Return the purée to the pan with the rest of the chickpeas and the remaining cooking water.

4 Heat the remaining olive oil in a frying pan. Add the chopped sun-dried tomatoes, rosemary and the remaining garlic cloves and cook gently, stirring frequently, until just golden. Remove and discard the rosemary and garlic.

5 Stir the sun-dried tomatoes with their flavoured oil into the chickpea mixture. Add the measured water and bring to the boil. Season to taste with salt and pepper. Stir in the pasta, and cook for about 10 minutes until it is just tender. Ladle the soup into warmed soup bowls and serve immediately with grated Parmesan cheese, if you like.

Chickpea Energy 309kcal/1297kJ; Protein 11.5g; Carbohydrate 35.1g, of which sugars 1.7g; Fat 14.6g, of which saturates 2.3g; Cholesterol 4mg; Calcium 60mg; Fibre 4.3g; Sodium 142mg.
Beetroot Swirl Energy 138kcal/587kJ; Protein 4g; Carbohydrate 31.4g, of which sugars 30.8g; Fat 0.5g, of which saturates 0g; Cholesterol 0mg; Calcium 63mg; Fibre 5.1g; Sodium 79mg.

Red Pepper Soup with Lime

The beautiful rich red colour of this soup makes it a very attractive appetizer or light lunch.

Serves 4–6
5ml/1 tsp olive oil
4 fresh red (bell) peppers, seeded and chopped
1 large onion, chopped
1 garlic clove, crushed
1 small red chilli, sliced
45ml/3 tbsp tomato purée (paste)
juice and finely grated rind of 1 lime
900ml/1½ pints/3¼ cups vegetable stock
salt and ground black pepper
toast, to garnish

1 Heat the oil in a pan over low heat. Add the peppers and onion, cover with a tight-fitting lid and cook, shaking the pan occasionally, for about 5 minutes, until softened.

2 Stir in the garlic, then add the chilli and tomato purée. Stir in half the stock and bring to the boil. Cover the pan again and simmer for 10 minutes.

3 Leave to cool slightly, then ladle the soup into a food processor or blender, in batches if necessary, and process to a purée. Return it to the rinsed-out pan, stir in the remaining stock, the lime rind and juice and season to taste with salt and pepper.

4 Bring the soup back to the boil, then ladle it into warmed soup bowls. Add a piece of toasted bread to each bowl and serve immediately.

> **Cook's Tip**
> *Small, pointed chillies are usually hotter than the larger, blunt ones. If you prefer a milder flavour, halve the chilli lengthways and scrape out the seeds and surrounding membrane with the blade of the knife before slicing. Most of the heat of chilli is concentrated in this membrane. Wash your hands well after handling it and avoid touching your eyes.*

Curried Parsnip Soup

The spices in this soup impart a delicious, mild curry flavour redolent of the days of the British Raj.

Serves 4
25g/1oz/2 tbsp butter
1 garlic clove, crushed
1 onion, chopped
5ml/1 tsp ground cumin
5ml/1 tsp ground coriander
450g/1lb (about 4) parsnips, sliced
10ml/2 tsp medium curry paste
450ml/¾ pint/scant 2 cups vegetable stock
450ml/¾ pint/scant 2 cups milk
60ml/4 tbsp sour cream
good squeeze of lemon juice
salt and ground black pepper
fresh coriander (cilantro) sprigs, to garnish
garlic and coriander naan bread, to serve

1 Heat the butter in a large pan over medium heat. Add the garlic and onion and cook, stirring occasionally, for 4–5 minutes, until lightly golden. Stir in the cumin and coriander and cook, stirring frequently, for a further 1–2 minutes.

2 Add the parsnips and stir until well coated with the butter, then stir in the curry paste, followed by the stock. Bring to the boil, then reduce the heat to low, cover the pan with a tight-fitting lid and simmer gently for 15 minutes, until the parsnips are tender.

3 Leave the soup to cool slightly, then ladle it into a blender or food processor, in batches if necessary, and process to a smooth purée.

4 Return the soup to the rinsed-out pan and stir in the milk. Heat gently for 2–3 minutes, then stir in 30ml/2 tbsp of the sour cream and lemon juice to taste. Season to taste with salt and pepper.

5 Ladle the soup into warmed bowls and top each serving with a spoonful of the remaining sour cream. Garnish with the coriander sprigs and serve immediately accompanied by the warmed, spicy naan bread.

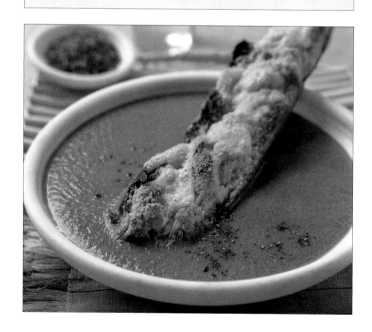

Green Pea & Mint Soup

This soup is equally delicious lightly chilled. Stir in the swirl of cream just before serving.

Serves 4
50g/2oz/4 tbsp butter
4 spring onions (scallions), chopped
450g/1lb/4 cups fresh or frozen peas

600ml/1 pint/2½ cups vegetable stock
2 large fresh mint sprigs
600ml/1 pint/2½ cups milk
pinch of sugar (optional)
salt and ground black pepper
single (light) cream and small fresh mint sprigs, to garnish

1 Heat the butter in a large pan over low heat. Add the spring onions and cook, stirring occasionally, for 3–5 minutes, until just softened but not coloured.

2 Stir the peas into the pan, add the stock and mint and bring to the boil. Cover and simmer very gently for about 30 minutes for fresh peas or 15 minutes if you are using frozen peas, until the peas are very tender. Remove about 45ml/3 tbsp of the peas using a slotted spoon and reserve for the garnish.

3 Leave the soup to cook slightly, then ladle it into a food processor or blender, add the milk and process until smooth. Return the soup to the rinsed-out pan and reheat gently. Season to taste with salt and pepper, adding a pinch of sugar if you like.

4 Ladle the soup into warmed bowls. Swirl a little cream into each, then garnish with mint and the reserved peas.

Cook's Tip
Fresh peas are increasingly available during the summer months from grocers and supermarkets. The time and effort of podding them are well worthwhile, as they impart a unique flavour to this delicious, vibrant soup.

Cream of Onion Soup

This wonderfully soothing soup has a buttery flavour that is complemented by crisp croûtons or chopped chives, sprinkled over just before serving.

Serves 4
115g/4oz/½ cup unsalted butter
1kg/2¼lb yellow onions, sliced

1 fresh bay leaf
105ml/7 tbsp dry white vermouth
1 litre/1¾ pints/4 cups good vegetable stock
150ml/¼ pint/⅔ cup double (heavy) cream
a little lemon juice (optional)
salt and ground black pepper
croûtons or chopped fresh chives, to garnish

1 Melt 75g/3oz/6 tbsp of the butter in a large heavy-based pan. Set about 200g/7oz of the onions aside and add the rest to the pan with the bay leaf. Stir to coat in the butter, then cover and cook very gently for about 30 minutes.

2 Add the vermouth, increase the heat and boil rapidly until the liquid has evaporated. Add the stock, 5ml/1 tsp salt and pepper to taste. Bring to the boil, lower the heat and simmer for 5 minutes, then remove from the heat. Leave to cool, then discard the bay leaf and process the soup in a blender or food processor. Return the soup to the rinsed pan.

3 Meanwhile, melt the remaining butter in another pan and cook the remaining onions slowly, covered, until soft but not browned. Uncover and continue to cook until golden yellow.

4 Add the cream to the soup and reheat it gently until hot, but do not allow it to boil. Taste and adjust the seasoning, adding a little lemon juice if liked. Add the buttery onions and stir for 1–2 minutes, then ladle the soup into bowls. Sprinkle with croûtons or chopped chives and serve.

Cook's Tip
Adding the second batch of onions gives texture and a buttery flavour to this soup. Make sure they do not brown.

Green Pea Energy 242kcal/1012kJ; Protein 12.1g; Carbohydrate 18.3g, of which sugars 10.5g; Fat 13.9g, of which saturates 8.4g; Cholesterol 36mg; Calcium 226mg; Fibre 5.9g; Sodium 247mg.
Onion Energy 519Kcal/2139kJ; Protein 3.8g; Carbohydrate 21.4g, of which sugars 15.6g; Fat 44.3g, of which saturates 27.5g; Cholesterol 113mg; Calcium 88mg; Fibre 3.5g; Sodium 193mg.

Country Vegetable Soup

To ring the changes with this soup, vary the vegetables according to what you like and what vegetables are in season.

Serves 4
50g/2oz/4 tbsp butter
1 onion, chopped
2 leeks, sliced
2 celery sticks, sliced
2 carrots, sliced
2 small turnips, chopped
4 ripe tomatoes, peeled and chopped
1 litre/1¾ pints/4 cups vegetable stock
1 bouquet garni
115g/4oz/1 cup green beans, chopped
salt and ground black pepper
chopped fresh herbs such as tarragon, thyme, chives and parsley, to garnish

1 Melt the butter in a large, heavy pan over low heat. Add the onion and leeks and cook gently, stirring occasionally, for about 8 minutes, until softened but not coloured.

2 Add the celery, carrots and turnips and cook, stirring occasionally, for 3–4 minutes. Stir in the tomatoes and stock, add the bouquet garni and simmer the vegetables gently for about 20 minutes.

3 Add the beans to the soup and continue to cook until all the vegetables are tender. Season to taste with salt and pepper.

4 Ladle the soup into warmed soup bowls, garnish with chopped fresh herbs and serve immediately.

Cook's Tip
You can use the cooking water from a wide variety of vegetables and pulses as a flavoursome, easy and economical vegetable stock. Equally, vegetable peelings work well. Carrots, cauliflower, broccoli, green beans, leeks, lettuce, mushrooms, onions and potatoes are all good choices, but you should be light-handed with cabbage and members of the cabbage family, such as Brussels sprouts.

Pasta & Dried Bean Soup

In Italy this soup is made with dried or fresh beans and served hot or at room temperature.

Serves 4–6
300g/11oz/1¼ cups dried borlotti or cannellini beans
400g/14oz can chopped plum tomatoes, with their juice
3 garlic cloves, crushed
2 bay leaves
90ml/6 tbsp olive oil, plus extra to serve
750ml/1¼ pints/3 cups water
10ml/2 tsp salt
200g/7oz/scant 2 cups ditalini or other small pasta
45ml/3 tbsp chopped fresh flat leaf parsley
ground black pepper
freshly grated Parmesan cheese, to serve

1 Place the beans in a bowl, add cold water to cover and leave to soak overnight. Drain the beans, rinse and drain well again.

2 Place the beans in a large pan and add water to cover. Bring to the boil and cook for 10 minutes. Drain, rinse and drain again, then return them to the pan. Add enough water to cover them by 2.5cm/1in. Stir in the tomatoes with their can juice, the garlic, bay leaves and olive oil and season with pepper. Bring to the boil, then lower the heat and simmer for 1½–2 hours, or until the beans are tender. Add more water during cooking if necessary to keep the beans covered.

3 Remove and discard the bay leaves. Pass about half of the bean mixture through a food mill or process to a purée in a food processor. Stir the purée into the pan with the remaining bean mixture. Add the measured water and bring the soup to the boil.

4 Add the salt and pasta. Stir, then cook until the pasta is just tender. Stir in the parsley.

5 Remove the pan from the heat and leave to stand for at least 10 minutes. Ladle the soup into warmed soup bowls and serve with extra olive oil for drizzling and grated Parmesan cheese for sprinkling.

Vegetable Energy 160kcal/665kJ; Protein 3.6g; Carbohydrate 11.5g, of which sugars 10g; Fat 11.4g, of which saturates 6.8g; Cholesterol 27mg; Calcium 72mg; Fibre 5.4g; Sodium 106mg.
Pasta Energy 360kcal/1518kJ; Protein 15.7g; Carbohydrate 49g, of which sugars 4.6g; Fat 12.6g, of which saturates 1.8g; Cholesterol 0mg; Calcium 78mg; Fibre 9.9g; Sodium 346mg.

Avocado Soup

This delicious soup has a fresh, delicate flavour and a wonderful colour. For added zest, add a generous squeeze of lime juice or spoon 15ml/1 tbsp salsa into the soup just before serving. Choose ripe avocados for this soup – they should feel soft when gently pressed. Keep very firm avocados at room temperature for 3–4 days. To speed ripening, place in a brown paper bag.

Serves 4
2 large ripe avocados
300ml/½ pint/1¼ cups
* sour cream*
1 litre/1¾ pints/4 cups
* well-flavoured vegetable stock*
small bunch of fresh
* coriander (cilantro)*
ground black pepper

1 Cut the avocados in half, remove the peel and lift out the stones (pits). Chop the flesh coarsely and place it in a food processor with 45–60ml/3–4 tbsp of the sour cream. Process until smooth.

2 Heat the vegetable stock in a pan. When it is hot, but still below simmering point, stir in the rest of the cream.

3 Gradually stir the avocado mixture into the hot stock. Heat but do not let the mixture approach boiling point.

4 Chop the coriander. Ladle the soup into individual heated bowls and sprinkle each portion with chopped coriander and black pepper. Serve immediately.

> **Cook's Tip**
> *Once cut, avocados should be used immediately as they have a tendency to discolour. If you need to prepare avocados ahead of time, toss them in lemon or lime juice and store in an airtight container in the refrigerator.*

Pears & Stilton

Firm juicy pears and piquant cheese are a truly magical combination in this summer appetizer – a perfect start to an al fresco meal.

Serves 4
4 ripe pears
75g/3oz blue Stilton cheese
50g/2oz/3 tbsp curd
* (farmer's) cheese*

salt and ground black pepper
fresh watercress sprigs or mizuna,
* to garnish*

For the dressing
45ml/3 tbsp light olive oil
15ml/1 tbsp lemon juice
10ml/2 tsp toasted poppy seeds

1 First make the dressing. Place the olive oil, lemon juice and poppy seeds in a screw-topped jar and season with salt and pepper. Close the lid and shake well until combined.

2 Cut the pears in half lengthways, then scoop out the cores and cut away the calyx from the rounded end.

3 Beat together the Stilton, curd cheese and a little pepper. Divide this mixture among the cavities in the pears. Arrange the filled pear halves on individual plates.

4 Shake the dressing to mix it again, then spoon it over the pears. Serve garnished with watercress or mizuna.

> **Cook's Tip**
> *The pears should be lightly chilled in the refrigerator before they are used in this dish.*

> **Variation**
> *Stilton is the classic British blue cheese used in this classic British dish but you could use blue Cheshire, Roquefort or Gorgonzola instead.*

Avocado Soup Energy 407kcal/1676kJ; Protein 3.3g; Carbohydrate 3.4g, of which sugars 2.1g; Fat 42.2g, of which saturates 21.7g; Cholesterol 78mg; Calcium 73mg; Fibre 3.2g; Sodium 24mg.
Pears Energy 243kcal/1007kJ; Protein 7.2g; Carbohydrate 15.5g, of which sugars 15.5g; Fat 17.2g, of which saturates 6.4g; Cholesterol 21mg; Calcium 109mg; Fibre 3.5g; Sodium 208mg.

Chinese Garlic Mushrooms

High in protein and low in fat, marinated tofu makes an unusual stuffing for these baked mushroom caps.

Serves 4
8 large open mushrooms
3 spring onions (scallions), sliced

1 garlic clove, crushed
30ml/2 tbsp oyster sauce
5g/1 0oz packet marinated
   tofu, diced
200g/7oz can corn, drained
10ml/2 tsp sesame oil
salt and ground black pepper

1 Preheat the oven to 200°C/400°F/Gas 6. Finely chop the mushroom stalks and mix with the next three ingredients.

2 Stir in the diced marinated tofu and corn, season well, then spoon the filling into the mushroom caps.

3 Brush the edges of the mushrooms with the sesame oil. Place them in an ovenproof dish and bake for 12–15 minutes, until the mushrooms are just tender, then serve immediately.

Ricotta & Borlotti Bean Pâté

A lovely, light yet full-flavoured vegetarian pâté.

Serves 4
400g/14oz can borlotti beans,
   drained and rinsed
175g/6oz/¾ cup ricotta cheese

1 garlic clove
60ml/4 tbsp melted butter
juice of ½ lemon
30ml/2 tbsp chopped
   fresh parsley
15ml/1 tbsp chopped fresh thyme
salt and ground black pepper

1 Put the beans, ricotta, garlic, butter and lemon juice in a food processor or blender and process. Add the parsley and thyme, season with salt and pepper and process again.

2 Spoon into a serving dish or four lightly oiled and base-lined ramekins. Chill. Garnish with salad leaves and serve with warm crusty bread or toast.

Tomato & Cheese Tarts

These crisp little tartlets are easier to make than they look and are best eaten fresh from the oven.

Serves 4
2 sheets filo pastry

1 egg white
115g/4oz/½ cup low-fat soft
   (farmer's) cheese
handful of fresh basil leaves
3 small tomatoes, sliced
salt and ground black pepper

1 Preheat the oven to 200°C/400°F/Gas 5. Brush the sheets of filo pastry lightly with egg white and, using a sharp knife, cut into sixteen 10cm/4in squares.

2 Layer the squares in pairs in eight patty tins (muffin pans). Spoon the cheese into the pastry cases (pie shells). Season with salt and ground black pepper and top with basil leaves.

3 Arrange the tomato slices on the tartlets, season with salt and pepper and bake for 10–12 minutes, until golden. Serve warm or at room temperature.

Cook's Tip

Filo pastry can be made at home but the process is quite laborious and takes a long time. It is much easier to buy chilled or frozen ready-made dough. The sheets should be kept covered until you are working on them. Brushing with melted butter, oil or egg white before baking makes sure that the layers are crisp.

Variations
• *Substitute crumbled goat's cheese or feta for the soft (farmer's) cheese or cut a goat's cheese log into eight slices.*
• *Use four red and four yellow cherry tomatoes, halved and in two-colour pairs, to decorate the tops of these tartlets.*
• *Sprinkle the tartlets with chopped fresh chives when they have been assembled.*

Mushrooms Energy 86kcal/361kJ; Protein 7.9g; Carbohydrate 4g, of which sugars 3.2g; Fat 4.4g, of which saturates 0.6g; Cholesterol 0mg; Calcium 268mg; Fibre 2.2g; Sodium 701mg.
Pâté Energy 290kcal/1208kJ; Protein 11g; Carbohydrate 19.3g, of which sugars 5.1g; Fat 19.3g, of which saturates 11.9g; Cholesterol 50mg; Calcium 74mg; Fibre 6.2g; Sodium 481mg.
Tarts Energy 118kcal/497kJ; Protein 7.3g; Carbohydrate 17.9g, of which sugars 3.6g; Fat 2.8g, of which saturates 1.6g; Cholesterol 7mg; Calcium 65mg; Fibre 1.3g; Sodium 149mg.

Avocados with Tangy Topping

Lightly grilled with a tasty topping of red onions and cheese, this dish makes a delightful appetizer.

Serves 4

15ml/1 tbsp sunflower oil
1 small red onion, sliced
1 garlic clove, crushed

dash of Worcestershire sauce
2 ripe avocados, halved and stoned (pitted)
2 small tomatoes, sliced
15ml/1 tbsp chopped fresh basil, marjoram or parsley
50g/2oz Lancashire or mozzarella cheese, sliced
salt and ground black pepper

1 Heat the oil in a frying pan over low heat. Add the onion and garlic and cook, stirring occasionally, for about 5 minutes, until just softened. Shake in a little Worcestershire sauce.

2 Preheat the grill (broiler). Place the avocado halves on the grill (broiling) pan and spoon the onion mixture into the centres. Divide the tomato slices and fresh herbs among the four halves and top with the cheese.

3 Season well with salt and pepper and grill (broil) until the cheese melts and starts to brown.

Chilled Avocado Salad

This simple appetizer makes a delightful change from avocados with vinaigrette.

Serves 4

2 avocados
juice of 1 lemon

300ml/½ pint/1¼ cups Greek (US strained plain) yogurt
2 garlic cloves, crushed
2 orange (bell) pepper, seeded and diced
salt and ground black pepper

1 Peel, halve and stone (pit) the avocados. Dice the flesh and toss with the lemon juice. Mix together the yogurt and garlic, season and fold in the avocados. Place in a serving dish, sprinkle with the orange peppers and chill before serving.

Bruschetta with Goat's Cheese

Simple to prepare in advance, this tempting dish can be served as an appetizer or as part of a finger buffet.

Serves 4–6
For the tapenade
400g/14oz black olives, pitted and finely chopped
50g/2oz sun-dried tomatoes in oil, drained and chopped
30ml/2 tbsp capers, rinsed and chopped
15ml/1 tbsp green peppercorns, in brine, crushed

2 garlic cloves, crushed
45ml/3 tbsp chopped fresh basil
45–60ml/3–4 tbsp olive oil
salt and ground black pepper

For the bases
12 slices ciabatta or other crusty bread
olive oil, for brushing
2 garlic cloves, halved
115g/4oz/½ cup soft goat's cheese or other full-fat soft cheese
mixed fresh herb sprigs, to garnish

1 To make the tapenade, mix all the tapenade ingredients together and check the seasoning. It should not need too much. Leave to marinate overnight, if possible.

2 To make the bruschetta, toast both sides of the bread lightly until golden. Brush one side of each slice with with oil and then rub with the garlic cloves. Set aside until ready to serve.

3 Spread the bruschetta with the cheese, fluffing it up with a fork, and spoon the tapenade on top. Garnish with sprigs of mixed fresh herbs.

> **Cook's Tips**
> • Grill the bruschetta on a barbecue for a delicious smoky flavour if you are making this appetizer in the summer.
> • Basil loses its characteristic flavour when dried – fresh basil is infinitely better. If the fresh herb is not available, you could substitute 15ml/1 tbsp good-quality pesto without sacrificing the flavour.

Avocados Energy 162kcal/668kJ; Protein 3.6g; Carbohydrate 2.9g, of which sugars 1.9g; Fat 15.1g, of which saturates 4.1g; Cholesterol 7mg; Calcium 56mg; Fibre 2.2g; Sodium 55mg.
Salad Energy 264kcal/1094kJ; Protein 7.7g; Carbohydrate 9.8g, of which sugars 7.3g; Fat 22.5g, of which saturates 7.1g; Cholesterol 0mg; Calcium 129mg; Fibre 4.3g; Sodium 62mg.
Bruschetta Energy 288kcal/1197kJ; Protein 8.1g; Carbohydrate 17.8g, of which sugars 1.5g; Fat 20.9g, of which saturates 5.8g; Cholesterol 18mg; Calcium 107mg; Fibre 2.8g; Sodium 1795mg.

Asparagus with Tarragon Butter

Eating fresh asparagus with your fingers is correct but messy, so serve this dish with finger bowls.

Serves 4
500g/1¼lb fresh asparagus
115g/4oz/½ cup butter
30ml/2 tbsp chopped
  fresh tarragon
15ml/1 tbsp chopped fresh flat
  leaf parsley
grated rind of ½ lemon
15ml/1 tbsp lemon juice
salt and ground black pepper

1 Trim off the woody ends from the asparagus spears, then tie the spears into four equal bundles.

2 Pour water into a large frying pan to a depth of about 2.5cm/1in and bring to the boil. Add the bundles of asparagus, cover with a lid and cook for 6–8 minutes, until the asparagus is tender but still firm. Drain well and discard the strings.

3 Arrange the asparagus spears on four warmed serving plates. Make the tarragon butter by creaming together the remaining ingredients. Heat the flavoured butter gently until just melted, then pour it over the asparagus. Serve immediately.

Cook's Tip
Frugal — and clever — cooks waste nothing. Add the trimmed woody ends of the asparagus spears to the cooking water and reserve the water when you drain the spears. Discard the woody ends. Use the cooking water to flavour home-made soups, such as asparagus or green pea soup.

Variation
You can also serve the asparagus with parsley and orange butter. Use 45ml/3 tbsp finely chopped fresh flat leaf parsley instead of the tarragon, substitute 10ml/2 tsp orange rind for the lemon rind and use orange instead of lemon juice.

Celeriac Fritters with Mustard Dip

The contrast of the hot, crisp fritters and the cold mustard dip makes this a very tasty combination.

1 celeriac (about 450g/1lb)
squeeze of lemon juice
oil, for deep-frying
salt and ground black pepper
sea salt flakes, for sprinkling

Serves 4
1 egg
115g/4oz/1 cup ground almonds
45ml/3 tbsp freshly grated
  Parmesan cheese
45ml/3 tbsp chopped fresh flat
  leaf parsley

For the mustard dip
150ml/¼ pint/⅔ cup sour cream
15–30ml/1–2 tbsp wholegrain
  mustard

1 Beat the egg well and pour into a shallow dish. Mix together the almonds, grated Parmesan and parsley in a separate dish. Season to taste, then set aside.

2 Peel and cut the celeriac into strips about 1cm/½in wide and 5cm/2in long. Immediately drop the strips into a bowl of water with a little lemon juice added to prevent them from becoming discoloured.

3 Heat the oil in a deep-fat fryer to 180°C/350°F or until a cube of day-old bread browns in 30 seconds. Drain and then pat dry half the celeriac strips. Dip them into the beaten egg, then into the ground almond mixture, making sure that the pieces are coated completely and evenly.

4 Deep-fry the celeriac fritters, a few at a time, for about 2–3 minutes, until golden. Drain on kitchen paper and keep warm while you cook the remainder.

5 To make the mustard dip, mix together the sour cream, mustard and salt to taste. Spoon into a small serving bowl.

6 Heap the celeriac fritters on to warmed individual serving plates. Sprinkle with sea salt flakes and serve immediately with the mustard dip.

Asparagus Energy 249kcal/1022kJ; Protein 4.1g; Carbohydrate 3g, of which sugars 2.8g; Fat 24.5g, of which saturates 15.1g; Cholesterol 61mg; Calcium 59mg; Fibre 2.6g; Sodium 179mg.
Fritters Energy 434kcal/1796kJ; Protein 14g; Carbohydrate 4.6g, of which sugars 3.8g; Fat 40.2g, of which saturates 10g; Cholesterol 81mg; Calcium 297mg; Fibre 3.6g; Sodium 288mg.

Garlic Mushrooms

Serve these on toast for a quick, tasty appetizer or pop them into ramekins and serve with slices of warm crusty bread.

Serves 4
450g/1lb button (white)
  mushrooms, sliced if large
45ml/3 tbsp olive oil
45ml/3 tbsp stock or water
30ml/2 tbsp dry sherry (optional)
3 garlic cloves, crushed
115g/4oz/1/2 cup low-fat
  soft (farmer's) cheese
30ml/2 tbsp chopped
  fresh parsley
15ml/1 tbsp chopped fresh chives
salt and ground black pepper
toast or bread, to serve

1 Put the mushrooms into a large pan with the olive oil, stock or water and sherry, if using. Heat until the liquid is bubbling, then cover the pan with a tight-fitting lid and simmer gently for about 5 minutes.

2 Add the crushed garlic and stir well to mix. Cook for a further 2 minutes. Remove the mushrooms with a slotted spoon and set them aside. Cook the liquid until it reduces to about 30ml/2 tbsp. Remove the pan from the heat and stir in the soft cheese, parsley and chives.

3 Stir the mixture well until the cheese has completely melted, then return the mushrooms to the pan and stir so that they become coated with the cheese mixture. Season to taste with salt and pepper.

4 Pile the mushrooms on to thick slabs of hot toast and serve immediately. Alternatively, spoon them into four ramekins and serve accompanied by slices of crusty bread.

> **Cook's Tip**
> Use a mixture of different types of mushrooms for this dish, if you like. Shiitake mushrooms, if you can find them, will give this appetizer a particularly rich flavour. Oyster mushrooms, on the other hand, offer an interesting texture.

Vegetables with Tahini

This colourful appetizer is easily prepared in advance. For an *al fresco* meal, you could grill the vegetables on a barbecue.

Serves 4
2 red, green or yellow (bell)
  peppers, seeded and quartered
2 courgettes (zucchini),
  halved lengthways
2 small aubergines
  (eggplants), halved lengthways
  and salted on the cut surface
1 fennel bulb, quartered
olive oil, for brushing
115g/4oz halloumi cheese, sliced
salt and ground black pepper
warm pitta or naan bread,
  to serve

For the tahini cream
225g/8oz tahini paste
1 garlic clove, crushed
30ml/2 tbsp olive oil
30ml/2 tbsp freshly squeezed
  lemon juice
120ml/4fl oz/1/2 cup cold water

1 Preheat the grill (broiler) or barbecue until hot. Pat dry the aubergines, then brush the vegetables with olive oil and cook until just browned, turning once. (If the peppers blacken and blister, don't worry. The skins can be peeled off when they are cool enough to handle.) Cook the vegetables until just soft.

2 Place all the vegetables in a shallow dish and season to taste with salt and pepper. Leave to cool slightly. They are best served warm rather than hot.

3 Meanwhile, brush the cheese slices with olive oil and grill (broil) these on both sides until they are just charred. Remove them from the grill (broiler) pan with a metal spatula.

4 To make the tahini cream, place all the ingredients, except the water, in a food processor or blender. Process for a few seconds to mix, then, with the motor still running, pour in the water and blend until smooth.

5 Place the vegetables and cheese slices on a platter and trickle over the tahini cream. Serve with plenty of warm pitta or naan bread while the cheese is still hot, as it will become rubbery as it cools down.

Mushrooms Energy 131kcal/542kJ; Protein 6.7g; Carbohydrate 1.8g, of which sugars 1.5g; Fat 11.3g, of which saturates 2.8g; Cholesterol 7mg; Calcium 65mg; Fibre 1.9g; Sodium 136mg.
Vegetables Energy 523kcal/2164kJ; Protein 19.1g; Carbohydrate 9.9g, of which sugars 9.1g; Fat 45.5g, of which saturates 9.7g; Cholesterol 17mg; Calcium 530mg; Fibre 9.1g; Sodium 136mg.

Sautéed Wild Mushrooms

This is a quick dish to prepare and makes an ideal side dish for all kinds of vegetarian main courses.

Serves 6
900g/2lb fresh mixed wild and cultivated mushrooms such as morels, porcini, chanterelles, oyster or shiitake

30ml/2 tbsp olive oil
25g/1oz/2 tbsp unsalted (sweet) butter
2 garlic cloves, chopped
3 or 4 shallots, finely chopped
45–60ml/3–4 tbsp chopped fresh parsley, or a mixture of different chopped fresh herbs
salt and ground black pepper

1 Wash and carefully dry the mushrooms. Trim the stems and cut the mushrooms into quarters, or slice if they are very large.

2 Heat the oil in a large frying pan over medium-hot heat. Add the butter and swirl to melt, then stir in the mushrooms and cook for 4–5 minutes until beginning to brown.

3 Add the garlic and shallots to the pan and cook for a further 4–5 minutes until the mushrooms are tender and any liquid given off has evaporated. Season to taste with salt and pepper and stir in the parsley or mixed herbs and serve hot.

Cook's Tip
Use as many different varieties of cultivated and wild mushrooms as you can find for a maximum taste.

Variation
For marinated mushrooms, fry 1 small chopped onion and 1 garlic clove in 30ml/2 tbsp olive oil. Stir in 15ml/1 tbsp tomato purée (paste) and 50ml/2fl oz/¼ cup dry white wine and a pinch of saffron threads. Season, cover and simmer gently for 45 minutes. Add 225g/8oz mushrooms, cover and cook for 5 minutes. Cool, still covered, then chill before serving.

Straw Potato Cake

This potato cake is so-named in France because of its resemblance to a woven straw doormat. But, of course, it tastes mouthwateringly good.

Serves 4
450g/1lb baking potatoes
22.5ml/1½ tbsp melted butter
15ml/1 tbsp vegetable oil
salt and ground black pepper

1 Peel the baking potatoes and grate them coarsely, then immediately toss them with the melted butter and season well with salt and pepper.

2 Heat the oil in a large frying pan. Add the potato mixture and press down to form an even layer that covers the base of the pan. Cook over medium heat for 7–10 minutes until the underside is well browned.

3 Loosen the potato cake by shaking the pan or running a thin palette knife under it.

4 To turn it over, invert a large baking sheet over the frying pan and, holding it tightly against the pan, turn them both over together. Lift off the frying pan, return it to the heat and add a little more oil if it looks dry. Slide the potato cake into the frying pan and continue cooking until it is crisp and browned on the second side. Serve immediately.

Cook's Tip
Make several small potato cakes instead of one large one, if you prefer. Simply adjust the cooking time.

Variation
Replace some of the potato with grated carrot or parsnip, or add some grated cheese and a pinch of freshly grated nutmeg to the raw potato and butter mix.

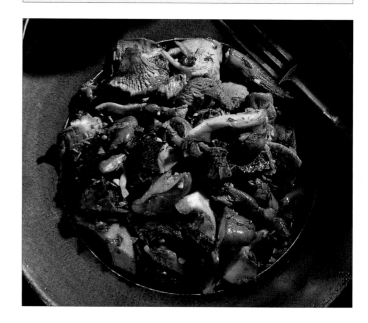

Potato Cake Energy 145kcal/609kJ; Protein 2g; Carbohydrate 18.2g, of which sugars 1.5g; Fat 7.7g, of which saturates 3.4g; Cholesterol 12mg; Calcium 8mg; Fibre 1.1g; Sodium 47mg.
Wild Mushrooms Energy 92kcal/381kJ; Protein 3.2g; Carbohydrate 2.2g, of which sugars 1.4g; Fat 8g, of which saturates 2.9g; Cholesterol 9mg; Calcium 29mg; Fibre 2.3g; Sodium 36mg.
Celeriac (opposite) Energy 41kcal/171kJ; Protein 1g; Carbohydrate 1.7g, of which sugars 1.7g; Fat 3.5g, of which saturates 2g; Cholesterol 8mg; Calcium 78mg; Fibre 2.1g; Sodium 135mg.

Celeriac Purée

Many chefs add potato to celeriac purée, but this recipe highlights the pure flavour of the vegetable.

Serves 4
1 large celeriac (about 800g/1¾ lb), peeled
15g/½ oz/1 tbsp butter
pinch of grated nutmeg
salt and ground black pepper

1 Cut the celeriac into large dice, put in a pan with enough cold water to cover and add a little salt. Bring to the boil over medium-hot heat and cook gently for about 10–15 minutes until tender.

2 Drain the celeriac, reserving a little of the cooking liquid, and place in a food processor fitted with a metal blade or a blender. Process until smooth, adding a little of the cooking liquid if the purée needs thinning.

3 Stir in the butter and season to taste with salt, pepper and nutmeg. Reheat, if necessary, before serving.

Hummus

This popular dish is widely available in supermarkets, but nothing compares to the home-made variety. It is very easy to make.

Serves 4–6
175g/6oz/1 cup cooked chickpeas
120ml/4fl oz/½ cup tahini paste
3 garlic cloves
juice of 2 lemons
45–60ml/3–4 tbsp water
salt and ground black pepper

1 Place the chickpeas, tahini paste, garlic, lemon juice, seasoning and a little of the water in a blender or food processor. Process until smooth, adding a little more water, if necessary. Chill before serving.

Cannellini Bean Purée

This easy dish is wonderful with warm pitta bread.

Serves 4
400g/14oz can cannellini beans, rinsed and drained
45ml/3tbsp fromage frais or cream cheese
grated rind and juice of 1 large orange
15ml/1 tbsp finely chopped fresh rosemary
4 heads chicory (Belgian endive), halved lengthways
2 radicchio, cut into 8 wedges
15ml/1 tbsp walnut oil

1 Purée the drained beans in a blender or food processor with the fromage frais, orange rind and juice and the rosemary.

2 Lay the chicory and radicchio on a baking tray and brush with the walnut oil. Grill (broil) for 2–3 minutes until beginning to brown. Serve immediately with the purée.

Creamy Spinach Purée

Crème fraîche or béchamel sauce usually gives this dish its creamy richness. Here is a quick light alternative.

Serves 4
675g/1½lb/6 cups leaf spinach, stems removed
115g/4oz/½ cup full or medium-fat soft cheese
milk (if required)
pinch of freshly grated nutmeg
salt and ground black pepper

1 Rinse the spinach, shake lightly and place in a deep frying pan or wok. Cook over medium heat for about 3–4 minutes until wilted. Drain in a colander, pressing with the back of a spoon. The spinach does not need to be completely dry.

2 Process the spinach and soft cheese in a food processor or blender to form a purée, then transfer to a bowl. If the purée is too thick, add a little milk. Season to taste with salt, pepper and nutmeg. Transfer to a heavy pan and reheat gently to serve.

Hummus Energy 303kcal/1282kJ; Protein 18.5g; Carbohydrate 44.7g, of which sugars 5.2g; Fat 6.9g, of which saturates 1.2g; Cholesterol 0mg; Calcium 88mg; Fibre 7.2g; Sodium 16mg.
Cannellini Energy 143kcal/602kJ; Protein 8.2g; Carbohydrate 20.5g, of which sugars 6.3g; Fat 3.6g, of which saturates 0.4g; Cholesterol 0mg; Calcium 96mg; Fibre 6.7g; Sodium 397mg.
Spinach Energy 94kcal/388kJ; Protein 7.4g; Carbohydrate 3.6g, of which sugars 3.4g; Fat 5.5g, of which saturates 2.8g; Cholesterol 12mg; Calcium 287mg; Fibre 3.6g; Sodium 236mg.

Braised Red Cabbage

Lightly spiced with a sharp-sweet flavour, this dish goes well with Spinach & Potato Galette or Onion Tart.

Serves 4–6
1kg/2lb red cabbage
2 onions, chopped
2 cooking apples, peeled, cored and grated
5ml/1 tsp freshly grated nutmeg
1.5ml/¼ tsp ground cloves
1.5ml/¼ tsp ground cinnamon
15g/½ oz/1 tbsp soft dark brown sugar
45ml/3 tbsp red wine vinegar
25g/1oz/2 tbsp butter or margarine, diced
salt and ground black pepper

1 Preheat the oven to 160°C/325°F/Gas 3. Cut away and discard the large white ribs from the outer cabbage leaves using a large sharp knife, then finely shred the cabbage.

2 Layer the shredded cabbage in a large ovenproof dish with the onions, apples, spices and sugar, seasoning with salt and pepper. Pour over the red wine vinegar and add the diced butter or margarine.

3 Cover the ovenproof dish and cook in the oven for about 1½ hours, stirring a couple of times, until the cabbage is very tender. Serve immediately.

Cook's Tips
• *This recipe can be cooked in advance. Bake the cabbage for 1½ hours, then cool. To complete the cooking, oven bake at the same temperature for about 30 minutes, stirring occasionally.*
• *Add a splash of red wine if the dish starts to look dry during cooking, then add a little extra sugar to taste.*

Variation
Try adding a strip of orange rind to the dish before cooking, then remove before serving.

Winter Vegetable Salad

This simple side salad is guaranteed to brighten up a winter menu. Made of leeks, cauliflower and celery, it is subtly flavoured with white wine, chopped herbs and juniper berries.

Serves 4
175ml/6 fl oz/¾ cup white wine
5ml/1 tsp olive oil
30ml/2 tbsp lemon juice
2 bay leaves
1 fresh thyme sprig
4 juniper berries
450g/1lb leeks, trimmed and cut into 2.5cm/1in lengths
1 small cauliflower, broken into florets
4 celery sticks, sliced on the diagonal
30ml/2 tbsp chopped fresh parsley
salt and ground black pepper

1 Put the wine, olive oil, lemon juice, bay leaves, thyme and juniper berries into a large, heavy pan and bring to the boil. Cover and leave to simmer 20 minutes.

2 Add the leeks, cauliflower and celery. Simmer very gently for 5–6 minutes, or until just tender.

3 Remove the vegetables with a slotted spoon and transfer them to a serving dish. Briskly boil the cooking liquid remaining in the pan for 15–20 minutes, or until reduced by half. Strain through a sieve (strainer).

4 Stir the parsley into the liquid and season to taste with salt and pepper. Pour over the vegetables and leave to cool. Chill for at least 1 hour before serving.

Cook's Tips
• *Using the stock as a dressing, and adding only a tiny amount of oil, means that this dish is ideal for anyone on a low-fat diet.*
• *Do not overcook the cauliflower: it should still feel firm to the bite. Remove the vegetables from the pan as they are done.*
• *Vary the vegetables for this salad according to taste: the cauliflower with broccoli and the celery with carrot sticks.*

Red Cabbage Energy 121kcal/508kJ; Protein 3.1g; Carbohydrate 19.4g, of which sugars 18.1g; Fat 3.9g, of which saturates 2.2g; Cholesterol 9mg; Calcium 98mg; Fibre 5g; Sodium 40mg.
Winter Salad Energy 101kcal/421kJ; Protein 6g; Carbohydrate 7.1g, of which sugars 5.8g; Fat 2.4g, of which saturates 0.4g; Cholesterol 0mg; Calcium 89mg; Fibre 5.2g; Sodium 35mg.

Lemony Carrots

The carrots are cooked until just tender in a lemony stock which is then thickened to make a light tangy sauce.

Serves 4

450g/1lb carrots, thinly sliced
bouquet garni
15ml/1 tbsp freshly squeezed lemon juice
pinch of freshly grated nutmeg
20g/¾ oz/1½ tbsp butter
15ml/½ oz/1 tbsp plain (all-purpose) flour
salt and ground black pepper

1 Bring 600ml/1 pint/2½ cups water to the boil in a large pan, then add the carrots, bouquet garni and lemon juice. Add a pinch of nutmeg and season to taste with salt and pepper.

2 Bring back to the boil, then lower the heat slightly and simmer until the carrots are tender. Remove the carrots using a slotted spoon, then keep warm.

3 Boil the cooking liquid hard until it has reduced to about 300ml/½ pint/1¼ cups. Discard the bouquet garni.

4 Mash 15g/½oz/1 tbsp of the butter and all of the flour together, then gradually whisk into the simmering reduced cooking liquid, whisking well after each addition. Continue to simmer for about 3 minutes, stirring frequently, until the sauce has thickened.

5 Return the carrots to the pan, heat through in the sauce, then remove from the heat. Stir in the remaining butter and serve immediately.

Cook's Tip
A bouquet garni is a small bunch of herbs, usually bay leaves, parsley and thyme, tied together with string or in a muslin bag. If you make your own, you can add different herbs to suit a dish. Dried bouquet garnis are sold in supermarkets.

Ratatouille

Bursting with Mediterranean flavours, this tasty dish may be served hot or cold, as a tasty starter, side dish or vegetarian main course.

Serves 4

2 large aubergines (eggplants), roughly chopped
150ml/¼ pint/⅔ cup olive oil
2 onions, sliced
2 garlic cloves, chopped
4 courgettes (zucchini), roughly chopped
1 large red (bell) pepper, seeded and roughly chopped
2 large yellow (bell) peppers, seeded and roughly chopped
1 fresh rosemary sprig
1 fresh thyme sprig
5ml/1 tsp coriander seeds, crushed
3 plum tomatoes, peeled, seeded and chopped
8 basil leaves, roughly torn
salt and ground black pepper
fresh parsley or basil sprigs, to garnish

1 Place the aubergines in a colander, sprinkle with salt and place a plate with a weight on top. Leave for 30 minutes to extract the bitter juices.

2 Heat the olive oil in a large pan and gently fry the onions for about 6–7 minutes until just softened. Add the garlic and cook for a further 2 minutes, stirring frequently.

3 Rinse the aubergines under cold running water, then drain and pat dry with kitchen paper. Add the aubergines to the pan of onions, together with the courgettes and peppers. Increase the heat and sauté for a few minutes until just turning brown.

4 Add the rosemary, thyme and coriander seeds, then cover the pan and cook gently for about 30 minutes.

5 Add the tomatoes and season to taste with salt and pepper. Cook gently for a further 10 minutes, until the vegetables are soft but not too mushy.

6 Remove the sprigs of herbs. Stir in the torn basil leaves and adjust the seasoning. Leave to cool slightly and serve warm or cold, garnished with sprigs of parsley or basil.

Carrots Energy 89kcal/372kJ; Protein 1.1g; Carbohydrate 11.8g, of which sugars 8.4g; Fat 4.5g, of which saturates 2.7g; Cholesterol 11mg; Calcium 34mg; Fibre 2.8g; Sodium 59mg.
Ratatouille Energy 349kcal/1442kJ; Protein 6.4g; Carbohydrate 21.6g, of which sugars 19.1g; Fat 26.9g, of which saturates 4g; Cholesterol 0mg; Calcium 82mg; Fibre 7.3g; Sodium 18mg.

Green Beans with Almond Butter

This dish is also a perfect accompaniment for baked or grilled oily fish.

Serves 4

350g/12oz green beans, trimmed
50g/2oz/¼ cup butter
50g/2oz/⅓ cup whole blanched almonds
grated (shredded) rind and juice of 1 unwaxed lemon
salt and ground black pepper

1 Cook the beans in a pan of salted, boiling water for about 3 minutes, or until just tender. Drain well. Meanwhile, melt the butter in a large non-stick pan until foamy.

2 Add the almonds to the pan and cook, stirring occasionally, for 2–3 minutes, or until golden. Remove from the heat and toss with the beans, lemon rind and juice. Season.

Parsnips with Almonds

Parsnips are sweetly spiced to bring out their flavour.

Serves 4

450g/1lb small parsnips
35g/1¼ oz/scant 3 tbsp butter
25g/1oz/¼ cup flaked (sliced) almonds
15g/½ oz/1 tbsp soft light brown sugar
pinch of ground mixed spice
15ml/1 tbsp lemon juice
salt and ground black pepper
chopped fresh chervil or parsley, to garnish

1 Cook the parsnips in boiling salted water until almost tender. Drain well. When the parsnips are cool enough to handle, cut each in half across its width, then quarter lengthways.

2 Melt the butter in a pan. Gently cook the parsnips and almonds, stirring and turning until they are lightly flecked with brown.

3 Mix together the sugar and spice, sprinkle over the parsnips and stir to mix. Trickle over the lemon juice. Season to taste with salt and pepper and heat for 1 minute. Garnish with herbs.

Turnips with Orange

Turnips coated in a delicious orange-flavoured buttery sauce make a wonderful alternative to the more usual potato side dish.

Serves 4

50g/2oz/¼ cup butter
15ml/1 tbsp vegetable oil
1 small shallot, finely chopped
450g/1lb small turnips, peeled and quartered
300ml/½ pint/1¼ cups freshly squeezed orange juice
salt and ground black pepper
roughly torn fresh flat leaf parsley, to garnish

1 Heat the butter and oil in a pan and cook the shallot gently, stirring occasionally, until softened but not coloured.

2 Add the turnips to the shallot and cook over medium heat, shaking the pan frequently, until the turnips start to absorb the butter and oil.

3 Pour the orange juice on to the turnips, turn to coat well, then simmer gently for about 30 minutes, until the turnips are tender and the orange juice is reduced to a buttery sauce. Season with salt and pepper, if required, then garnish with parsley and serve immediately.

> **Cook's Tips**
> • Sprinkle toasted nuts, such as flaked (sliced) almonds or chopped walnuts, over the turnips to add a contrast in textures.
> • Use tender, young turnips, available in early summer. They have creamy coloured flesh and skins tinged with purple or green.

> **Variation**
> Use a mixture of parsnips and carrots; cut into large chunks and add 10ml/2 tsp soft light brown sugar with the orange juice to bring out the sweetness of the vegetables.

Green Beans Energy 191kcal/786kJ; Protein 4.4g; Carbohydrate 3.7g, of which sugars 2.6g; Fat 17.7g, of which saturates 7.2g; Cholesterol 27mg; Calcium 64mg; Fibre 2.9g; Sodium 78mg.
Parsnips Energy 190kcal/794kJ; Protein 3.4g; Carbohydrate 18.5g, of which sugars 10.7g; Fat 11.9g, of which saturates 5.1g; Cholesterol 19mg; Calcium 65mg; Fibre 5.7g; Sodium 66mg.
Turnips Energy 176kcal/732kJ; Protein 1.7g; Carbohydrate 13.2g, of which sugars 12.6g; Fat 13.5g, of which saturates 6.9g; Cholesterol 27mg; Calcium 68mg; Fibre 3g; Sodium 101mg.

Red Cabbage with Pears & Nuts

A sweet and sour, spicy red cabbage dish, with the added juiciness of pears and extra crunch of walnuts.

Serves 6

15ml/1 tbsp walnut oil
1 onion, sliced
2 whole star anise
5ml/1 tsp ground cinnamon
pinch of ground cloves
450g/1lb red cabbage, finely
  shredded
25g/1oz/2 tbsp soft dark
  brown sugar
45ml/3 tbsp red wine vinegar
300ml/½ pint/1¼ cups red wine
150ml/¼ pint/⅔ cup port
2 pears, cut into 1cm/½in cubes
115g/4oz/⅔ cup raisins
115g/4oz/1 cup walnut halves
salt and ground black pepper

1 Heat the oil in a large heavy pan. Add the sliced onion and cook over low heat, stirring occasionally, for about 5 minutes until softened.

2 Add the star anise, cinnamon, cloves and cabbage and cook for about 3 minutes more.

3 Stir in the sugar, vinegar, red wine and port. Cover the pan and simmer gently for 10 minutes, stirring occasionally.

4 Stir in the cubed pears and raisins and cook without replacing the lid for a further 10 minutes, or until the cabbage is tender. Season to taste with salt and pepper. Mix in the walnut halves and serve immediately.

> **Cook's Tip**
> The vinegar and wine help to preserve the beautiful colour of the cabbage as well as adding to the flavour.

> **Variation**
> Omit the star anise and cinnamon and add 15ml/1 tbsp juniper berries with the ground cloves.

Swiss Soufflé Potatoes

A fabulous combination of rich and satisfying ingredients – cheese, eggs, cream, butter and potatoes. This is the perfect dish for cold-weather entertaining.

Serves 4

4 baking potatoes, about
  900g/2lb total weight
115g/4oz/1 cup grated
  Gruyère cheese
115g/4oz/½ cup herb butter
60ml/4 tbsp double (heavy)
  cream
2 eggs, separated
salt and ground black pepper
snipped fresh chives, to garnish

1 Preheat the oven to 220°C/425°F/Gas 7. Scrub the potatoes, then prick them all over with a fork. Bake for 1–1½ hours until tender. Remove them from the oven and reduce the temperature to 180°C/350°F/Gas 4.

2 Cut each potato in half and scoop out the flesh into a bowl. Place the potato shells on a baking sheet and return them to the oven to crisp up while you are making the filling.

3 Mash the potato flesh, then add the Gruyère cheese, herb butter, cream and egg yolks. Beat well until smooth, then season to taste with salt and pepper.

4 Whisk the egg whites until stiff peaks form, then carefully fold into the potato mixture. Pile the mixture into the potato shells and bake for 20–25 minutes until risen and golden brown.

5 Transfer the potatoes to a warmed serving dish, garnish with chives and serve immediately.

> **Cook's Tip**
> To make the herb butter, mix 45ml/3 tbsp finely chopped fresh parsley and 10ml/2 tsp finely chopped fresh dill with 115g/4oz/½ cup softened butter. Season with a little salt.

Red Cabbage Energy 202kcal/847kJ; Protein 1.8g; Carbohydrate 30.1g, of which sugars 29.8g; Fat 2.1g, of which saturates 0.2g; Cholesterol 0mg; Calcium 60mg; Fibre 3.2g; Sodium 23mg.
Potatoes Energy 585kcal/2431kJ; Protein 14.3g; Carbohydrate 32.7g, of which sugars 3.1g; Fat 44.5g, of which saturates 27.2g; Cholesterol 205mg; Calcium 251mg; Fibre 2g; Sodium 443mg.

Thai Noodle Salad

The coconut milk and sesame oil in the dressing gives this salad an unusual nutty flavour.

Serves 4
350g/12oz somen noodles
1 large carrot, cut into thin strips
1 bunch of asparagus, trimmed and cut into 4cm/1½in lengths
1 red (bell) pepper, seeded and cut into fine strips
115g/4oz mangetouts (snow peas), trimmed and halved
115g/4oz baby corn, halved lengthways
115g/4oz/2 cups beansprouts
115g/4oz can water chestnuts, drained and finely sliced
1 lime, cut into wedges

50g/2oz roasted peanuts, roughly chopped
fresh coriander (cilantro) leaves

For the dressing
45ml/3 tbsp roughly torn fresh basil
75ml/5 tbsp roughly chopped fresh mint
250ml/8fl oz/1 cup coconut milk
30ml/2 tbsp dark sesame oil
15ml/1 tbsp grated fresh root ginger
2 garlic cloves, finely chopped
juice of 1 lime
2 spring onions (scallions), finely chopped
salt and cayenne pepper

1 To make the dressing mix the basil, mint, coconut milk, sesame oil, ginger, garlic, lime juice and spring onions. Season with salt and cayenne pepper.

2 Cook the noodles in a pan of boiling water until just tender, following the directions on the packet. Drain, rinse under cold running water and drain again.

3 Cook the carrot, asparagus, pepper, mangetouts and baby corn cobs in a large pan of boiling water until tender, but still crisp. Drain, plunge them immediately into cold water and then drain again.

4 Toss the noodles, vegetables and dressing together until well combined and coated with the dressing.

5 Arrange on individual serving plates and garnish with the lime wedges, peanuts and coriander leaves.

Cauliflower with Three Cheeses

The mingled flavours of three cheeses give a new twist to cauliflower cheese. Serve with roasted cherry tomatoes and chunks of hot olive bread for an elegant meat-free meal.

Serves 4
4 baby cauliflowers
250ml/8fl oz/1 cup single (light) cream
75g/3oz dolcelatte cheese, diced
75g/3oz mozzarella cheese, diced
45ml/3 tbsp freshly grated Parmesan cheese
pinch of freshly grated nutmeg
ground black pepper
toasted breadcrumbs, to garnish

1 Cook the cauliflowers in a large pan of boiling salted water for 8–10 minutes until just tender.

2 Meanwhile, put the cream in a small pan with the cheeses. Heat gently until the cheeses have melted, stirring occasionally. Season to taste with nutmeg and pepper.

3 When the cauliflowers are cooked, drain them thoroughly and place one on each of four warmed plates.

4 Carefully spoon a little of the cheese sauce over each cauliflower and sprinkle each with a few of the toasted breadcrumbs. Serve immediately.

Cook's Tips
• *For a more economical dish or if baby cauliflowers are not available, use one large cauliflower instead. Cut it into quarters with a large sharp knife and remove the central core.*
• *The luxurious sauce is very simple to make as it does not use a butter and flour base like a conventional cheese sauce. To make the sauce slightly less rich, replace the cream with milk.*
• *To make the toasted breadcrumbs, use bread that is a couple of days old and turn into crumbs in a food processor. Toast until golden, shaking often. You could also use chopped nuts instead.*

Potato Gnocchi with Hazelnut Sauce

These delicate Italian potato dumplings are dressed with a wonderful, creamy-tasting hazelnut sauce.

Serves 4
675g/1½ lb large potatoes
115g/4oz/1 cup plain
  (all-purpose) flour, plus
  extra for dusting

For the hazelnut sauce
115g/4oz/½ cup hazelnuts,
  roasted
1 garlic clove, roughly chopped
½ tsp grated lemon rind
½ tsp lemon juice
30ml/2 tbsp sunflower oil
150g/5oz/¾ cup low-fat
  fromage frais
salt and ground black pepper

1 To make the sauce, put just over half of the hazelnuts in a blender or food processor with the garlic, grated lemon rind and juice. Process until coarsely chopped. With the motor running, gradually add the oil until the mixture is smooth. Spoon into a heatproof bowl and mix in the fromage frais. Season to taste with salt and pepper.

2 Put the potatoes in a pan of cold water. Bring to the boil and cook for 20–25 minutes. Drain well. When cool enough to handle, peel them and pass through a food mill into a bowl.

3 Add the flour a little at a time, until the mixture is smooth and slightly sticky. Add salt to taste. Roll out the mixture on to a floured board to form a sausage 1cm/½in in diameter. Cut into 2cm/¾in lengths. Roll one piece at at time on a floured fork to make the characteristic ridges. Flip on to a floured plate or tray.

4 Cook a batch of gnocchi in a large pan of boiling water for 3–4 minutes. Lift out with a slotted spoon and keep hot while cooking the rest of the gnocchi in the same way.

5 To heat the sauce, place the bowl over a pan of simmering water and heat gently, being careful not to let it curdle. Pour the sauce over the gnocchi. Roughly chop the remaining hazelnuts, scatter them over the top and serve immediately.

Winter Vegetable Hot-pot

Made with a variety of root vegetables, this one-pot dish is richly flavoured, and substantial enough to make a vegetarian main course.

Serves 4
2 onions, sliced
4 carrots, sliced
1 small swede, sliced
2 parsnips, sliced
3 small turnips, sliced
½ celeriac, cut into matchsticks
2 leeks, thinly sliced
30ml/2 tbsp mixed chopped fresh
  herbs, such as parsley and
  thyme
1 garlic clove, chopped
1 bay leaf, crumbled
300ml/½ pint/1¼ cups vegetable
  stock
15g/½ oz/1 tbsp plain
  (all-purpose) flour
675g/1½ lb red-skinned
  potatoes, scrubbed and
  thinly sliced
50g/2oz/¼ cup butter
salt and ground black pepper

1 Preheat the oven to 190°C/375°F/Gas 5. Arrange all the vegetables, except the potatoes, in layers in a large casserole with a tight-fitting lid, seasoning them lightly with salt and pepper and sprinkling them with chopped fresh herbs, garlic and crumbled bay leaf as you go.

2 Blend the vegetable stock into the flour and pour over the vegetables. Arrange the potatoes in overlapping layers on top. Dot with butter and cover tightly.

3 Cook in the oven for 1¼ hours, or until the vegetables are tender. Remove the lid from the casserole and cook for a further 15–20 minutes until the top layer of potatoes is golden and crisp at the edges. Serve immediately.

> **Cook's Tips**
> • Make sure the root vegetables are cut into even-size slices so they cook uniformly.
> • For cheesy toasts to serve with the hot-pot, toast slices of French bread on one side. Turn over and sprinkle the other side with grated Gruyère cheese, then grill (broil) until golden.

Gnocchi Energy 495kcal/2071kJ; Protein 11.9g; Carbohydrate 52.9g, of which sugars 5.3g; Fat 27.6g, of which saturates 4.3g; Cholesterol 3mg; Calcium 132mg; Fibre 4.5g; Sodium 35mg.
Hot-Pot Energy 367kcal/1542kJ; Protein 8.5g; Carbohydrate 58.2g, of which sugars 24.5g; Fat 12.8g, of which saturates 7g; Cholesterol 27mg; Calcium 203mg; Fibre 13.1g; Sodium 178mg.

Vegetable Ribbons

This elegant vegetable side dish looks very impressive.

Serves 4

3 carrots
3 courgettes (zucchini)
120ml/4fl oz/½ cup vegetable
  stock
30ml/2 tbsp freshly chopped
  parsley
salt and ground black pepper

1 Using a vegetable peeler or sharp knife, cut the carrots and courgettes into thin ribbons.

2 Bring the vegetable stock to the boil in a pan and add the carrots. Return the stock to the boil, then add the courgettes. Boil rapidly for 2–3 minutes, or until the vegetable ribbons are just tender. Stir in the chopped parsley, season lightly with salt and ground black pepper and serve immediately.

Runner Beans with Tomatoes

Try to use tender young beans for this dish. If you use older ones, you will need to remove the "strings" down the sides before cooking.

Serves 4

675g/1½ lb/2 cups sliced runner
  (green) beans
40g/1½oz/3 tbsp butter
4 ripe tomatoes, peeled and
  chopped
salt and ground black pepper
chopped fresh tarragon, to garnish

1 Bring a pan of water to the boil, add the beans, return to the boil and cook for 3 minutes. Drain well.

2 Heat the butter in a pan, add the tomatoes and beans and season with salt and pepper. Cover the pan with a tight-fitting lid and simmer gently for about 10–15 minutes until tender.

3 Turn the beans and tomatoes into a warm serving dish, garnish with tarragon and serve immediately.

Rosemary Roasties

These potatoes are roasted with their skins on, giving them far more flavour than traditional roast potatoes. They are the ideal accompaniment to a nut roast.

Serves 4

1kg/2lb small red potatoes
30ml/2 tbsp olive oil
30ml/2 tbsp fresh rosemary
  leaves
pinch of paprika
salt

1 Leave the potatoes whole with the skins on, or if large, cut in half. Place the potatoes in a large pan of cold water and bring to the boil, then drain immediately.

2 Meanwhile, preheat the oven to 240°C/475°F/Gas 9.

3 Return the potatoes to the pan and drizzle the oil over them. Shake the pan to coat the potatoes evenly in the oil.

4 Transfer the potatoes to a roasting pan. Sprinkle with the rosemary, paprika and salt, then roast in the oven for 30 minutes, until the potatoes are golden brown and crisp; turn them once during cooking so that they brown evenly.

5 Remove the roasties from the oven, drain on kitchen paper and serve immediately.

> **Cook's Tip**
> The potatoes can be cut into smaller wedges, in which case the boiling stage can be omitted. Serve wedges with mayonnaise as an alternative to chips, or offer as canapés with drinks.

> **Variation**
> Add about 10 unpeeled garlic cloves to the roasting pan with the potatoes, adding a little extra oil and tossing well to coat. Roast the garlic with the potatoes; they will develop a sweet taste.

Ribbons Energy 42kcal/175kJ; Protein 2g; Carbohydrate 7.4g, of which sugars 6.9g; Fat 0.7g, of which saturates 0.2g; Cholesterol 0mg; Calcium 39mg; Fibre 2.5g; Sodium 183mg.
Runner Beans Energy 129kcal/536kJ; Protein 3.5g; Carbohydrate 8.6g, of which sugars 7.9g; Fat 9.2g, of which saturates 5.5g; Cholesterol 21mg; Calcium 65mg; Fibre 4.4g; Sodium 70mg.
Roasties Energy 189kcal/801kJ; Protein 4.3g; Carbohydrate 40.3g, of which sugars 3.3g; Fat 2.3g, of which saturates 0.4g; Cholesterol 0mg; Calcium 15mg; Fibre 2.5g; Sodium 28mg.

Stir-fried Broccoli with Soy Sauce & Sesame Seeds

This delicious side dish has an irresistible oriental flavour. Purple sprouting broccoli has been used for this recipe, but when it is not available an alternative variety of broccoli, such as calabrese, will also work very well. Serve with basmati rice and tofu.

Serves 2
225g/8oz purple
  sprouting broccoli
15ml/1 tbsp olive oil
15ml/1 tbsp soy sauce
15ml/1 tbsp toasted
  sesame seeds
salt and ground black pepper

1 Using a sharp knife, cut off and discard any thick stems from the broccoli and cut the broccoli into long, thin florets.

2 Heat the olive oil in a wok or large frying pan and add the broccoli. Stir-fry for 3–4 minutes, or until tender, adding a splash of water if the pan becomes too dry.

3 Add the soy sauce to the broccoli, then season with salt and ground black pepper to taste. Add sesame seeds, toss to combine and serve immediately.

Cook's Tip
Other vegetables from the brassica family could be substituted for broccoli, such as cauliflower, which can be prepared in the same way. Alternatively, try some shredded cabbage or pak choi (bok choy) or Brussels sprouts.

Variation
An essential part of the Asian diet for centuries, seaweed is now acknowledged in other parts of the world for its amazing health benefits. Try making this recipe with shredded nori, laver or arame.

Spring Onions with Dip

These spring onions go wonderfully well with the spicy dip.

Serves 6
3 bunches of plump spring onions (scallions), or Chinese green onions, which are about 2.5cm/1in across the bulb
olive oil, for brushing

For the romesco sauce
2–3 dried red chillies, such as Mexican anchos or guajillos

1 large red (bell) pepper, halved and seeded
2 large tomatoes, halved and seeded
4–6 large garlic cloves, unpeeled
75–90ml/5–6 tbsp olive oil
25g/1oz/¼ cup hazelnuts, blanched
4 slices French bread, each about 2cm/¾in thick
15ml/1 tbsp sherry vinegar
squeeze of lemon juice (optional)
chopped fresh parsley, to garnish

1 Prepare the sauce. Soak the dried chillies in hot water for about 30 minutes. Preheat the oven to 220°C/425°F/Gas 7. Place the pepper, tomatoes and garlic on a baking sheet and drizzle with 15ml/1 tbsp olive oil. Roast, uncovered, for 30–40 minutes, until the pepper is blistered and blackened. Cool slightly, then peel the pepper, tomatoes and garlic.

2 Heat the remaining oil in a small frying pan and fry the hazelnuts until lightly browned, then transfer them to a plate. Fry the bread in the same oil until light brown on both sides, then transfer to the plate with the nuts and leave to cool. Reserve the oil from cooking.

3 Drain the chillies, discard as many of their seeds as you can. Place the chillies in a food processor with the red pepper halves, tomatoes, garlic, hazelnuts and bread chunks, the reserved olive oil, and the vinegar. Process to a paste.

4 Trim the roots from the spring onions or trim the Chinese onion leaves so that they are about 15–18cm/6–7in long. Brush with oil. Heat an oiled ridged grill pan and cook the onions for about 2 minutes on each side, turning once and brushing with oil. Serve immediately with the sauce.

Broccoli and Sesame Energy 135kcal/558kJ; Protein 6.6g; Carbohydrate 2.7g, of which sugars 2.3g; Fat 10.9g, of which saturates 1.7g; Cholesterol 0mg; Calcium 115mg; Fibre 3.5g; Sodium 545mg.
Spring Onions Energy 212Kcal/886kJ; Protein 4.9g; Carbohydrate 20.7g, of which sugars 5.1g; Fat 12.8g, of which saturates 1.7g; Cholesterol 0mg; Calcium 58mg; Fibre 2.6g; Sodium 172mg.

Mushrooms with Chipotle Chillies

Chipotle chillies are *jalapeños* that have been smoke-dried. They are the perfect foil for the mushrooms in this simple warm salad. Serve with lots of warm bread to soak up the tasty juices.

Serves 6
2 chipotle chillies
450g/1lb/6 cups button (white) mushrooms
60ml/4 tbsp vegetable oil
1 onion, finely chopped
2 garlic cloves, chopped
fresh coriander (cilantro), to garnish

1 Soak the dried chillies in a bowl of hot water for about 10 minutes. Drain, then trim and remove the seeds. Chop finely.

2 Cut the mushrooms in half, if large. Heat the oil in a large frying pan. Add the onion, garlic, chillies and mushrooms and stir to coat in the oil. Fry for 6–8 minutes until the onion has softened. Transfer to a warmed dish. Chop some of the coriander, leaving some whole leaves, and use to garnish.

Baked Fennel with Parmesan

The delicate aniseed flavour of fennel is delicious with the sharpness of Parmesan cheese. Try serving with pasta dishes and risottos.

Serves 4–6
900g/2lb fennel bulbs, washed and cut in half
50g/2oz/¼ cup butter
40g/1½ oz/½ cup freshly grated Parmesan cheese

1 Cook the fennel bulbs in a large pan of boiling water until softened but not mushy. Drain well. Preheat the oven to 200°C/400°F/Gas 6.

2 Cut the fennel bulbs lengthways into four or six pieces. Place them in a buttered baking dish. Dot with butter, then sprinkle with the grated Parmesan. Bake in the oven for about 20 minutes until the cheese is golden brown. Serve immediately.

Courgettes with Sun-dried Tomatoes

Sun-dried tomatoes have a concentrated sweet flavour that goes particularly well with courgettes.

Serves 6
10 sun-dried tomatoes, dry or preserved in oil and drained
175ml/6fl oz/¾ cup warm water

75ml/5 tbsp olive oil
1 large onion, finely sliced
2 garlic cloves, finely chopped
900g/2lb courgettes (zucchini), cut into thin strips
salt and ground black pepper

1 Slice the sun-dried tomatoes into thin strips. Place in a bowl with the warm water. Allow to stand for 20 minutes.

2 Heat the oil in a large frying pan or pan, add the onion and cook over low to medium heat, stirring, until it has softened and turned translucent.

3 Stir in the garlic and the courgettes. Cook for about a further 5 minutes, continuing to stir the mixture.

4 Stir in the tomatoes and their soaking liquid. Season to taste with salt and pepper. Increase the heat slightly and cook until the courgettes are just tender. Serve hot or cold.

> **Cook's Tip**
> *Sprinkle with grated Parmesan just before serving, if you wish.*

> **Variation**
> *For courgettes in rich tomato sauce, cook the courgettes up to the end of step 3, then add one 400g/14oz can drained chopped tomatoes and 4 peeled and chopped fresh tomatoes. Stir in 5ml/1 tsp vegetable bouillon powder and 30ml/2tbsp tomato purée (paste). Simmer for 10–15 minutes, until the sauce has thickened. Season with salt and pepper and serve.*

Mushrooms Energy 83kcal/341kJ; Protein 2g; Carbohydrate 1.2g, of which sugars 0.8g; Fat 7.8g, of which saturates 0.9g; Cholesterol 0mg; Calcium 12mg; Fibre 1g; Sodium 5mg.
Baked Fennel Energy 96kcal/397kJ; Protein 3g; Carbohydrate 0.7g, of which sugars 0.6g; Fat 9.1g, of which saturates 5.7g; Cholesterol 24mg; Calcium 90mg; Fibre 0.8g; Sodium 127mg.
Courgettes Energy 141kcal/580kJ; Protein 3.2g; Carbohydrate 5.9g, of which sugars 4.9g; Fat 11.7g, of which saturates 1.7g; Cholesterol 0mg; Calcium 47mg; Fibre 2g; Sodium 4mg.

Broccoli Cauliflower Gratin

Broccoli and cauliflower look and taste good when served together, and this dish is much lighter than a classic cauliflower cheese.

Serves 4

1 small cauliflower (weighing about 250g/9oz)
1 head broccoli (weighing about 250g/9oz)
120ml/4fl oz/½ cup natural (plain) low-fat yogurt
75g/3oz/¼ cup grated reduced-fat Cheddar cheese
5ml/1 tsp wholegrain mustard
30ml/2 tbsp wholemeal (wholewheat) breadcrumbs
salt and ground black pepper

1 Break the cauliflower and broccoli into florets and cook in lightly salted boiling water for 8–10 minutes, until just tender. Drain well and arrange in a flameproof dish.

2 Preheat the grill (broiler) to medium hot. Mix together in a bowl the yogurt, grated cheese and mustard. Season the mixture to taste with pepper and spoon over the cauliflower and broccoli florets.

3 Sprinkle the breadcrumbs over the top of the dish and place under the grill until golden brown. Serve immediately.

Cook's Tip
When preparing the cauliflower and broccoli, discard the tougher parts of the stalks, then break the florets into even-size pieces so they will cook evenly.

Variations
Chopped nuts make a good alternative to breadcrumbs in this light dish; almonds, hazelnuts or walnuts would all be suitable. For non-vegetarians, try adding chopped ham before topping with the sauce, but this will increase the saturated fat content.

Potatoes Baked with Tomatoes

This dish from the south of Italy is utterly delicious, yet simplicity itself to make – mouthwatering layers of vegetables and cheese, baked until meltingly tender.

Serves 6

2 large red or yellow onions, thinly sliced
900g/2¼ lb potatoes, thinly sliced
450g/1lb fresh tomatoes, or canned, with their juice, sliced
90ml/6 tbsp olive oil
115g/4oz/1 cup freshly grated Parmesan or mature Cheddar cheese
few sprigs of fresh basil
salt and ground black pepper

1 Preheat the oven to 180°C/350°F/Gas 4. Brush a large baking dish generously with oil.

2 Arrange a layer of onions in the dish, followed by layers of potatoes and tomatoes. Pour on a little of the oil and sprinkle with cheese. Season with salt and pepper.

3 Repeat until the vegetables are used up, ending with an overlapping layer of potatoes and tomatoes. Tear the basil leaves into pieces, then add them here and there among the vegetables. Sprinkle the top with cheese and a little oil.

4 Pour on 50ml/2fl oz/¼ cup water. Bake for 1 hour, or until tender. If the top begins to brown too much, place a sheet of foil on top of the dish during cooking.

Cook's Tip
When ripe, flavourful tomatoes are available, use these instead of the canned variety; the resulting dish will be delicious and have a more authentic Italian flavour.

Variation
Add chopped garlic to the onions for a really robust flavour.

Gratin Energy 137kcal/573kJ; Protein 13.5g; Carbohydrate 11.1g, of which sugars 5g; Fat 4.5g, of which saturates 2.3g; Cholesterol 8mg; Calcium 273mg; Fibre 2.9g; Sodium 218mg.
Potatoes Energy 309kcal/1290kJ; Protein 9.8g; Carbohydrate 31.7g, of which sugars 8g; Fat 16.7g, of which saturates 4.9g; Cholesterol 15mg; Calcium 211mg; Fibre 3.2g; Sodium 189mg.

Aubergine Baked with Cheeses

The key to this speciality of southern Italy is a good home-made tomato sauce.

Serves 4–6
900g/2lb aubergines (eggplants), thinly sliced
flour, for coating
olive oil, for frying and greasing
40g/1½ oz/½ cup freshly grated Parmesan cheese

400g/14oz mozzarella cheese, sliced very thinly
salt and ground black pepper

For the tomato sauce
60ml/4 tbsp olive oil
1 onion, very finely chopped
1 garlic clove, chopped
450g/1lb fresh tomatoes, or canned, chopped, with the juice
few fresh basil or parsley sprigs

1 Layer the aubergine slices in a colander, sprinkling each layer with a little salt. Leave to drain for about 20 minutes, then rinse under cold running water and pat dry with kitchen paper.

2 To make the tomato sauce, cook the onion in the oil until translucent. Stir in the garlic and the tomatoes (if using fresh tomatoes, add 45ml/3 tbsp water). Season to taste with salt and pepper, then add the basil or parsley. Simmer gently for 30 minutes, stirring occasionally. Purée in a food mill, if you wish.

3 Pat the aubergine slices dry, then coat them lightly in flour. Heat a little oil in a large non-stick frying pan. Add a single layer of aubergines, cover and cook over low to medium heat until softened. Turn and cook on the other side. Remove from the pan with a slotted spoon and repeat with the remaining slices.

4 Preheat the oven to 180°C/350°F/Gas 4. Grease a wide shallow baking dish. Spread a little tomato sauce in the base. Cover with a layer of aubergine. Sprinkle with a few teaspoons of Parmesan, season to taste with salt and pepper, and cover with a layer of mozzarella. Spoon on some tomato sauce.

5 Repeat until all the ingredients are used up, ending with a covering of the tomato sauce and a sprinkling of Parmesan. Sprinkle with a little olive oil, and bake for about 45 minutes until golden and bubbling.

Baked Onions

One of the oldest and most widely used flavouring vegetables, the onion, also deserves to be used more as a vegetable in its own right. Onions become sweet and mildly flavoured when slowly boiled or baked, and can be cooked very conveniently in the oven when baking potatoes or roasting parsnips. Not only do they make a tasty accompaniment to many dishes, but they also have a range of health benefits.

Serves 4
4 large even-sized onions

1 Preheat the oven to 180°C/350°F/Gas 4. Put a little cold water into a medium-size roasting pan, and arrange the unpeeled onions in it.

2 Bake in the preheated oven for about 1 hour, or until the onions feel soft when squeezed at the sides. Peel the skins and serve immediately.

Cook's Tip
These onions are baked in their skins, but you could peel them, if preferred, before baking. The peeled onions are best baked in a covered casserole dish instead of a roasting tin.

Variation
Sweet-sour roasted onions are a delicious variation on the onion theme. Cut 4 large onions into wedges, leaving them attached at the root end. Preheat the oven to 200°C/400°F/Gas 6. Put the onions in a roasting tin and pour over 60ml/4 tbsp olive oil. Sprinkle 10ml/2 tsp crushed coriander seeds and mix thoroughly. Season, then roast for 20 minutes. Mix 15ml/1 tbsp honey with 30ml/2 tbsp pomegranate molasses, 15ml/1 tbsp sherry vinegar and 15ml/1 tbsp water. Drizzle over and stir. Reduce heat to 180°C/350°F/Gas 4 and cook for another 20–30 minutes.

Aubergine Energy 345kcal/1433kJ; Protein 17.2g; Carbohydrate 7.7g, of which sugars 5.9g; Fat 27.6g, of which saturates 12.3g; Cholesterol 45mg; Calcium 347mg; Fibre 3.9g; Sodium 346mg.
Baked Onions Energy 90kcal/375kJ; Protein 3g; Carbohydrate 19.8g, of which sugars 14g; Fat 0.5g, of which saturates 0g; Cholesterol 0mg; Calcium 63mg; Fibre 3.5g; Sodium 8mg.

Baby Leaf Salad with Croûtons

Crispy croûtons, made from Italian ciabatta bread, give a lovely crunch to this mixed leaf and avocado salad.

Serves 4

15ml/1 tbsp olive oil
1 garlic clove, crushed
15ml/1 tbsp freshly grated
  Parmesan cheese
15ml/1 tbsp chopped fresh
  parsley
4 slices ciabatta bread, crusts
  removed, cut into small dice
1 large bunch watercress
1 large handful of rocket (arugula)
1 bag mixed baby salad leaves,
  including oakleaf and cos
  lettuce
1 ripe avocado

For the dressing

45ml/3 tbsp olive oil
15ml/1 tbsp walnut oil
juice of 1/2 lemon
2.5ml/1/2 tsp Dijon mustard
salt and ground black pepper

1 Preheat the oven to 190°C/375°F/Gas 5. Put the oil, garlic, Parmesan, parsley and bread in a bowl and toss to coat well. Spread out the diced bread on a baking sheet and bake for about 8 minutes until crisp. Leave to cool.

2 Remove any coarse or discoloured stalks or leaves from the watercress and place in a serving bowl with the rocket and baby salad leaves.

3 Halve the avocado and remove the stone (pit). Peel and cut into chunks, then add it to the salad bowl.

4 To make the dressing, mix together the oils, lemon juice, mustard and salt and pepper to taste in a small bowl or screw-top jar until evenly blended. Pour over the salad and toss well. Sprinkle over the croûtons and serve at once.

> **Cook's Tip**
> Walnut oil adds a lovely nutty flavour to the dressing, but if you do not have any, just use olive oil only and add 15ml/1 tbsp balsamic vinegar instead of the lemon juice, if you prefer.

Wild Rice with Grilled Vegetables

A colourful array of summer vegetables, served on wild and white rice tossed in a garlicky dressing, provides a lovely main-course salad.

Serves 4

225g/8oz/1 1/4 cups wild and long
  grain rice mixture
1 large aubergine (eggplant),
  thickly sliced
1 red, 1 yellow and 1 green
  (bell) pepper, seeded and cut
  into quarters
2 red onions, sliced
225g/8oz brown cap or shiitake
  mushrooms
2 small courgettes (zucchini), cut
  in half lengthways
olive oil, for brushing
30ml/2 tbsp chopped fresh thyme

For the dressing

90ml/6 tbsp extra virgin olive oil
30ml/2 tbsp balsamic vinegar
2 garlic cloves, crushed
salt and ground black pepper

1 Put the rice mixture in a pan of cold salted water. Bring to the boil, reduce the heat, cover with a tight-fitting lid and cook gently for 30–40 minutes or according to the packet instructions, until all the grains are tender.

2 To make the dressing, mix together the olive oil, vinegar, garlic and salt and pepper to taste in a small bowl or screw-top jar until well blended. Set aside while you cook the vegetables.

3 Arrange the vegetables on a grill (broiler) rack. Brush with olive oil and grill (broil) for 8–10 minutes, until tender and well browned, turning them occasionally and brushing again with oil.

4 Drain the rice and toss in half the dressing. Turn into a serving dish and arrange the grilled vegetables on top. Pour over the remaining dressing and sprinkle over the chopped fresh thyme.

> **Cook's Tip**
> Wild rice is not a rice at all, but is actually a type of wild grass. It has a wonderfully nutty flavour and also adds attractive texture when mixed with long grain rice.

Baby Leaf Energy 334kcal/1397kJ; Protein 9.7g; Carbohydrate 26.9g, of which sugars 2.1g; Fat 21.6g, of which saturates 4g; Cholesterol 4mg; Calcium 238mg; Fibre 3.2g; Sodium 348mg.
Wild Rice Energy 438kcal/1824kJ; Protein 8.6g; Carbohydrate 60.3g, of which sugars 13.6g; Fat 18.1g, of which saturates 2.7g; Cholesterol 0mg; Calcium 56mg; Fibre 5.1g; Sodium 12mg.

Leeks with Mustard Dressing

Leeks are turned into an unusual and truly delicious salad when married with a mustardy dressing.

Serves 4

8 slim leeks, each about
    13cm/5in long
5–10ml/1–2 tsp Dijon mustard
10ml/2 tsp white wine vinegar
1 hard-boiled egg, halved
    lengthways
75ml/5 tbsp light olive oil
10ml/2 tsp chopped fresh parsley
salt and ground black pepper

1 Place the leeks in a steamer over a pan of boiling water and cook until they are just tender.

2 Meanwhile, stir together the mustard and vinegar in a bowl. Scoop the egg yolk into the bowl and, using a fork, mash thoroughly into the vinegar mixture.

3 Gradually work in the oil to make a smooth sauce, then season to taste with salt and pepper.

4 Lift the leeks out of the steamer and place on several layers of kitchen paper, then cover the leeks with several more layers of kitchen paper and dry.

5 Transfer the leeks to a serving dish while still warm, spoon the dressing over them and allow to cool. Finely chop the egg white using a large sharp knife, then mix with the chopped fresh parsley and scatter over the leeks. Chill before serving.

Cook's Tips

• Pencil-slim baby leeks are increasingly available nowadays, and are beautifully tender. Use three or four of these smaller leeks per serving.

• It is important that the leeks are thoroughly dried before placing in the serving dish, and they should still be warm when the dressing is added so that they absorb all the flavours.

Lettuce, Cucumber & Herb Salad

For a really quick salad, look out for pre-packed bags of mixed baby lettuce leaves in the supermarket.

Serves 4

½ cucumber
mixed lettuce leaves
1 bunch watercress, weighing
    about 115g/4oz
1 chicory (Belgian endive)
    head, sliced
45ml/3 tbsp mixed chopped fresh
    herbs such as parsley, thyme,
    tarragon, chives and chervil

For the dressing
15ml/1 tbsp white wine vinegar
5ml/1 tsp Dijon mustard
75ml/5 tbsp olive oil
salt and ground black pepper

1 Peel the cucumber, if you wish, then cut it in half lengthways and scoop out the seeds. Thinly slice the flesh. Tear the lettuce leaves into bite-size pieces.

2 Toss the cucumber, lettuce, watercress, chicory and herbs together in a large salad bowl, or arrange them in the bowl in layers, if you prefer.

3 To make the dressing, mix the vinegar and mustard together, then whisk in the oil and season with salt and pepper.

4 Stir the dressing and pour over the salad. Toss lightly to coat the salad vegetables and leaves and serve immediately.

Cook's Tip
Do not dress the salad until just before serving, otherwise the lettuce leaves will wilt.

Variation
To turn the salad into a light lunch dish, toss in some cubes of feta cheese and toasted pine nuts.

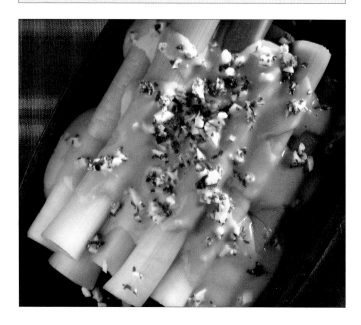

Leeks Energy 162kcal/670kJ; Protein 3.1g; Carbohydrate 2.5g, of which sugars 1.9g; Fat 15.7g, of which saturates 2.4g; Cholesterol 48mg; Calcium 48mg; Fibre 2.2g; Sodium 23mg.
Lettuce Energy 149kcal/612kJ; Protein 2.1g; Carbohydrate 2.7g, of which sugars 2.1g; Fat 14.6g, of which saturates 2.2g; Cholesterol 0mg; Calcium 100mg; Fibre 2g; Sodium 21mg.

Goat's Cheese Salad

The robust flavours of the goat's cheese and buckwheat combine especially well with figs and walnuts in this salad.

Serves 4
175g/6oz/1 cup couscous
30ml/2 tbsp toasted buckwheat
1 hard-boiled egg
4 ripe figs
30ml/2 tbsp chopped fresh parsley

60ml/4 tbsp olive oil, preferably Sicilian
45ml/3 tbsp walnut oil
115g/4oz rocket (arugula)
1/2 frisée lettuce, separated into leaves
175g/6oz crumbly white goat's cheese
50g/2oz/1/2 cup broken walnuts, toasted

1 Place the couscous and buckwheat in a bowl, cover with boiling water and leave to soak for 15 minutes. Place in a sieve (strainer), if necessary, to drain off any remaining water, then spread out on a metal tray and allow to cool.

2 Shell the hard-boiled egg and pass it through a fine grater. Trim the figs and almost cut each into four, leaving the pieces joined at the base.

3 Toss together the egg, parsley and couscous in a bowl. Mix together the two oils and use half to moisten the couscous and buckwheat mixture.

4 Put the lettuce leaves in a bowl and dress with the remaining oil, then divide among four large plates.

5 Pile the couscous into the centre of the leaves, crumble on the goat's cheese, scatter with toasted walnuts, and add the trimmed figs. Serve immediately.

> **Cook's Tip**
> *Serve this strongly flavoured salad with a gutsy red wine from the Rhône or South of France.*

Sweet Potato & Carrot Salad

A medley of colours, this warm salad not only looks great but has a fabulous sweet-and-sour flavour.

Serves 4
1 sweet potato
2 carrots, cut into thick diagonal slices
3 tomatoes
8–10 iceberg lettuce leaves
75g/3oz/1/2 cup canned chickpeas, drained

For the dressing
15ml/1 tbsp clear honey
90ml/6 tbsp natural (plain) yogurt
2.5ml/1/2 tsp salt
5ml/1 tsp ground black pepper

For the garnish
15ml/1 tbsp walnuts
15ml/1 tbsp sultanas (golden raisins)
1 small onion, cut into rings

1 Peel the sweet potato and cut roughly into cubes. Boil it until it is soft but not mushy, then drain and set aside.

2 Boil the carrots for just a few minutes, making sure that they remain crunchy. Drain the carrots and mix with the sweet potato in a large bowl.

3 Slice the tops off the tomatoes, then scoop out the seeds with a spoon and discard. Roughly chop the flesh. Slice the lettuce into strips across the leaves.

4 Line a salad bowl with the shredded lettuce leaves. Mix the chickpeas and tomatoes with the sweet potato and carrots, then place in the centre of the lettuce.

5 To make the dressing, put the honey and yogurt in a bowl with salt and pepper to taste, then mix well, using a fork. Garnish the salad with the walnuts, sultanas and onion rings. Pour the dressing over the top just before serving.

> **Variation**
> *Use baby new potatoes instead of the sweet potato cubes.*

Goat's Cheese Energy 595kcal/2469kJ; Protein 18g; Carbohydrate 38.7g, of which sugars 12.3g; Fat 41.8g, of which saturates 11.3g; Cholesterol 88mg; Calcium 243mg; Fibre 3.3g; Sodium 381mg.
Sweet Potato Energy 158kcal/669kJ; Protein 4.8g; Carbohydrate 27.7g, of which sugars 16.6g; Fat 4g, of which saturates 0.6g; Cholesterol 0mg; Calcium 94mg; Fibre 4.4g; Sodium 101mg.

Chicory, Fruit & Nut Salad

Mildly bitter chicory is
wonderful with sweet fruit,
and is delicious when
complemented by a creamy
curry sauce.

Serves 4
45ml/3 tbsp mayonnaise
15ml/1 tbsp Greek-style (US
    strained, plain) yogurt

15ml/1 tbsp mild curry paste
90ml/6 tbsp single (light) cream
$^1\!/_2$ iceberg lettuce
2 heads chicory (Belgian endive)
50g/2oz/1 cup flaked coconut
50g/2oz/$^1\!/_2$ cup cashew nuts
2 red eating apples
75g/3oz/$^1\!/_2$ cup currants

1 Mix together the mayonnaise, Greek-style yogurt, curry paste
and single cream in a small bowl. Cover and chill until required.

2 Tear the iceberg lettuce into even-size pieces and put into a
salad bowl.

3 Cut the root end off each head of chicory and discard. Slice
the chicory, or separate the leaves, and add to the salad bowl.
Preheat the grill (broiler).

4 Spread out the coconut flakes on a baking sheet. Grill (broil)
for 1 minute until golden. Turn into a bowl and set aside. Toast
the cashew nuts for 2 minutes until golden.

5 Quarter the apples and cut out the cores. Slice the apple
quarters and add to the lettuce with the toasted coconut,
cashew nuts and currants.

6 Stir up the chilled dressing and pour over the salad. Toss
lightly together and serve immediately.

Cook's Tip
*Choose a sweet, well-flavoured variety of red apple for this
salad, such as Royal Gala. Leave on the skins to provide added
colour and texture.*

Spicy Sweetcorn Salad

This brilliant, sweet-flavoured
salad is served warm with a
delicious, spicy dressing.

Serves 4
30ml/2 tbsp vegetable oil
450g/1lb drained canned
    sweetcorn, or frozen sweetcorn,
    thawed
1 green (bell) pepper, seeded and
    diced
1 small red chilli, seeded and finely
    diced

4 spring onions (scallions), sliced
45ml/3 tbsp chopped fresh
    parsley
225g/8oz cherry tomatoes, halved
salt and ground black pepper

For the dressing
2.5ml/$^1\!/_2$ tsp sugar
30ml/2 tbsp white wine vinegar
2.5ml/$^1\!/_2$ tsp Dijon mustard
15ml/1 tbsp chopped fresh basil
15ml/1 tbsp mayonnaise
1.5ml/$^1\!/_4$ tsp chilli sauce

1 Heat the oil in a frying pan. Add the sweetcorn, green
pepper, chilli and spring onions. Cook over medium heat for
about 5 minutes, until softened, stirring frequently.

2 Transfer the vegetables to a salad bowl. Stir in the parsley and
the cherry tomatoes.

3 To make the dressing, combine all the ingredients in a small
bowl and whisk together.

4 Pour the dressing over the sweetcorn mixture. Season with
salt and pepper to taste. Toss well to combine, then serve
immediately, while the salad is still warm.

Cook's Tip
Don't touch your eyes with your hands while preparing the chilli.

Variation
*If serving the salad to children, you can make the flavour milder
by omitting the fresh chilli and the chilli sauce.*

Chicory Energy 323kcal/1347kJ; Protein 5.7g; Carbohydrate 22.5g, of which sugars 19.8g; Fat 24.1g, of which saturates 8.7g; Cholesterol 21mg; Calcium 105mg; Fibre 4g; Sodium 122mg.
Sweetcorn Energy 245kcal/1032kJ; Protein 4.7g; Carbohydrate 35.9g, of which sugars 16.6g; Fat 10.2g, of which saturates 1.4g; Cholesterol 3mg; Calcium 39mg; Fibre 3.6g; Sodium 338mg.

Fennel & Orange Salad

This light and refreshing salad originated in Sicily, following the old custom of serving fennel at the end of a meal, to help digestion. The delicate aniseed flavour of the fennel marries well with sweet oranges.

Serves 4
2 large fennel bulbs (about 675g/1½ lb total)
2 sweet oranges
2 spring onions (scallions), to garnish

For the dressing
60ml/4 tbsp extra virgin olive oil
30ml/2 tbsp fresh lemon juice
salt and ground black pepper

1 Wash the fennel bulbs and remove any brown or stringy outer leaves. Slice the bulbs and stems into thin pieces. Place in a shallow serving bowl.

2 Peel the oranges with a sharp knife, cutting away the white pith. Slice thinly. Cut each slice into thirds. Arrange over the fennel, adding any juice from the oranges.

3 To make the dressing, mix the oil and lemon juice together. Season with salt and pepper. Pour the dressing over the salad and mix well.

4 Slice the white and green sections of the spring onions thinly. Sprinkle over the salad and serve immediately.

> **Cook's Tips**
> • For a delicate orange rind garnish to enhance the flavour of the salad, use a vegetable peeler to cut thin strips of rind from the unpeeled oranges, leaving the pith behind. Then cut the pieces into thin matchstick strips and cook in a small pan of boiling water for 2–3 minutes. Drain and dry on kitchen paper, then sprinkle on top of the salad before serving.
> • When buying fennel, choose firm round bulbs. The outer layers should be crisp and white, with the texture of green celery.

Tomato & Bread Salad

This salad is a traditional peasant dish from Tuscany and was created to use up bread that was several days old. The success of the dish depends on the quality of the tomatoes – they must be ripe and well flavoured. Serve with a green salad for a good contrast in colour and texture.

Serves 4
400g/14oz stale white or brown bread or rolls
4 large tomatoes
1 large red onion, or 6 spring onions (scallions)
a few fresh basil leaves, to garnish

For the dressing
60ml/4 tbsp extra virgin olive oil
30ml/2 tbsp white wine vinegar
salt and ground black pepper

1 Cut the bread or rolls into thick slices. Place in a shallow bowl and add enough cold water to soak the bread. Leave for at least 30 minutes.

2 Cut the tomatoes into chunks and place in a serving bowl. Finely slice the onion or spring onions and add them to the tomatoes. Squeeze as much water out of the bread as possible. Add the bread to the vegetables.

3 To make the dressing, whisk the olive oil with the vinegar, then season with salt and pepper.

4 Pour the dressing over the salad and mix well. Decorate with the basil leaves. Allow to stand in a cool place for a least 2 hours before serving.

> **Cook's Tip**
> Tomatoes left to ripen on the vine will have the best flavour so try to buy "vine-ripened" varieties. If you can only find unripened tomatoes, you can help them along by putting them in a paper bag with a ripe tomato or leaving them in a fruit bowl with a banana; the gases the ripe fruits give off will ripen them, but, unfortunately, this process cannot improve the flavour.

Tomato Energy 369kcal/1557kJ; Protein 9.7g; Carbohydrate 56.4g, of which sugars 8.5g; Fat 13.3g, of which saturates 1.7g; Cholesterol 0mg; Calcium 130mg; Fibre 3.2g; Sodium 531mg.
Fennel Energy 148kcal/614kJ; Protein 2.5g; Carbohydrate 9.6g, of which sugars 9.4g; Fat 11.4g, of which saturates 1.6g; Cholesterol 0mg; Calcium 78mg; Fibre 5.4g; Sodium 23mg.

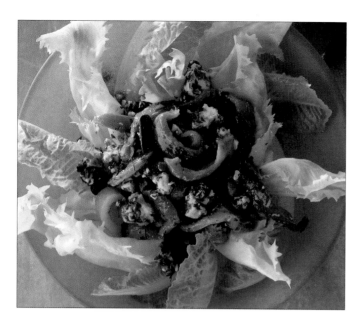

Grilled Mixed Peppers

Soft smoky grilled peppers make a lovely combination with the slightly tart salsa.

Serves 4
4 medium (bell) peppers in
    different colours
45ml/3 tbsp chopped fresh
    flat leaf parsley

For the salsa
45ml/3 tbsp chopped fresh dill
45ml/3 tbsp chopped fresh mint

1 small red onion, finely chopped
15ml/1 tbsp capers, rinsed and
    coarsely chopped
50g/2oz/¼ cup Greek olives,
    pitted and sliced
1 fresh green chilli, seeded and
    finely chopped
60g/4 tbsp pistachios, chopped
75ml/5 tbsp extra virgin olive oil
45ml/3 tbsp fresh lime juice
115g/4oz medium-fat feta
    cheese, crumbled
25g/1oz gherkins, finely chopped

1 Preheat the grill (broiler). Place the whole peppers on a baking sheet and grill (broil), turning occasionally with tongs, until charred and blistered.

2 Using tongs transfer the peppers to a plastic bag, tie the top and leave to cool.

3 When the peppers are cool enough to handle, peel and seed them and cut the flesh into even strips.

4 To make the salsa, mix all the ingredients together in a bowl and stir in the pepper strips. Serve at room temperature. If you are not going to serve immediately, cover the bowl with clear film (plastic wrap) and store in the refrigerator.

Cook's Tip
Placing the charred (bell) peppers in a sealed plastic bag to cool causes condensation, which helps to loosen the skins. An equally good method is to place the charred peppers in a bowl, cover with crumpled kitchen paper and leave to cool. If you are in a hurry, you can peel them as soon as they're cool enough to handle – it's just a bit more awkward.

Vegetable & Tofu Kebabs

A colourful mixture of vegetables and tofu, skewered, glazed and grilled until tender.

Serves 4
1 yellow (bell) pepper
2 small courgettes (zucchini)
225g/8oz piece of firm tofu
8 cherry tomatoes

6 button (white) mushrooms
15ml/1 tbsp wholegrain mustard
15ml/1 tbsp clear honey
30ml/2 tbsp olive oil
salt and ground black pepper
lime wedges and flat leaf parsley,
    to garnish
cooked mixed rice and wild rice,
    to serve

1 Preheat the grill (broiler). Cut the pepper in half and remove the seeds. Cut each half into quarters and then cut each quarter in half.

2 Trim the courgettes and then cut each courgette into seven or eight chunks.

3 Cut the tofu into 4cm/1½in pieces. Use a sharp knife to avoid squashing it and breaking it up.

4 Thread the pepper pieces, courgette chunks, tofu, cherry tomatoes and mushrooms alternately on to four long or eight shorter metal or bamboo skewers. (If you are using bamboo skewers, soak them in a bowl of cold water first. This will prevent them from charring during cooking.)

5 Whisk together the mustard, honey and olive oil in a small bowl. Season to taste with salt and pepper.

6 Put the kebabs on to a baking sheet. Brush them with the mustard and honey glaze. Cook under the grill for 8 minutes, turning once or twice during cooking and brushing with any remaining glaze.

7 Transfer the skewers to warmed plates and garnish with lime wedges and flat leaf parsley. Serve immediately with a mixture of long grain and wild rice.

Peppers Energy 364kcal/1504kJ; Protein 9.8g; Carbohydrate 13.6g, of which sugars 12.6g; Fat 30.3g, of which saturates 7.4g; Cholesterol 20mg; Calcium 193mg; Fibre 5.4g; Sodium 790mg.
Kebabs Energy 139kcal/575kJ; Protein 7.1g; Carbohydrate 8.7g, of which sugars 8.2g; Fat 8.6g, of which saturates 1.3g; Cholesterol 0mg; Calcium 318mg; Fibre 1.9g; Sodium 8mg.

Soufflé Omelette

This delectable fluffy omelette is light and delicate enough to melt in the mouth.

Serves I
2 eggs, separated
30ml/2 tbsp cold water

15ml/1 tbsp chopped fresh
   coriander (cilantro)
7.5ml/1½ tsp olive oil
30ml/2 tbsp mango chutney
25g/1oz/¼ cup grated
   Jarlsberg cheese
salt and ground black pepper

I Beat the egg yolks together with the cold water and coriander in a bowl and season with salt and pepper.

2 Whisk the egg whites in another grease-free bowl until stiff peaks form, then gently fold them into the egg yolk mixture with a rubber spatula.

3 Heat the oil in a frying pan, pour in the egg mixture and reduce the heat. Do not stir. Cook until the omelette becomes puffy and golden brown on the underside (carefully lift one edge with a spatula to check).

4 Spoon the chutney over the omelette and sprinkle with the Jarlsberg. Fold over and slide on to a warmed plate. Serve immediately. (If you like, place the pan under a hot grill/broiler to set the top before adding the chutney and cheese.)

Cook's Tip
If there is any trace of grease – and that includes any yolk – egg whites will not foam when whisked. It's best to use a glass, china or metal bowl. Plastic is easily scratched and then traces of grease are almost impossible to remove. The perfect choice is a copper bowl as the egg whites react with the metal to create a full and stable foam. However, do not leave the whisked whites to stand in a copper bowl, as they will turn grey. Whatever the material, the bowl should be a generous size to allow plenty of room for whisking.

Cheese Bubble & Squeak

This London breakfast dish was originally made on Mondays with leftover vegetables from the previous Sunday's lunch.

Serves 4
about 450g/1lb/3 cups mashed
   potatoes
about 225g/8oz/4 cups shredded
   cooked cabbage or kale

1 egg, lightly beaten
115g/4oz/1 cup grated
   Cheddar cheese
pinch of freshly grated nutmeg
salt and ground black pepper
plain (all-purpose) flour,
   for coating
vegetable oil, for frying

I Mix together the mashed potatoes, cabbage or kale, egg, cheese and nutmeg in a bowl and season with salt and pepper. Divide the mixture into eight pieces and shape into patties.

2 Place the patties on a large plate, cover with clear film (plastic wrap) and chill in the refrigerator for 1 hour or or more, if possible, as this helps firm up the mixture.

3 Gently toss the patties in the flour to coat lightly. Heat about 1cm/½in oil in a frying pan until it is quite hot.

4 Carefully slide the patties into the oil and cook for about 3 minutes on each side, until golden and crisp. Remove with a slotted spatula, drain on kitchen paper and serve hot and crisp.

Variation
For traditional bubble and squeak, heat 30ml/2 tbsp vegetable oil in a frying pan. Add 1 finely chopped onion and cook over low heat, stirring occasionally, for about 5 minutes, until softened but not coloured. Using a slotted spoon, transfer the onion to a bowl and mix with the other ingredients in step 1, omitting the cheese and using finely chopped cooked cabbage or Brussels sprouts. Use the same frying pan, with additional oil, for cooking the patties in step 4.

Omelette Energy 377kcal/1570kJ; Protein 19g; Carbohydrate 14.9g, of which sugars 14.8g; Fat 27g, of which saturates 9.2g; Cholesterol 405mg; Calcium 249mg; Fibre 0.3g; Sodium 648mg.
Bubble & Squeak Energy 281kcal/1175kJ; Protein 11.6g; Carbohydrate 21g, of which sugars 4.3g; Fat 16.7g, of which saturates 7.4g; Cholesterol 75mg; Calcium 254mg; Fibre 2.3g; Sodium 242mg.

Aubergine & Red Pepper Pâté

This simple pâté of baked aubergine, pink peppercorns and red peppers has more than a hint of garlic.

Serves 4

3 aubergines (eggplants)
2 large red (bell) peppers
5 garlic cloves, unpeeled
7.5ml/1½ tsp pink peppercorns
　　in brine, drained and crushed
30ml/2 tbsp chopped fresh
　　coriander (cilantro)
mixed salad leaves, to serve

1 Preheat the oven to 200°C/400°F/Gas 6. Arrange the whole aubergines, peppers and garlic cloves on a baking sheet and bake for 10 minutes. Transfer the garlic cloves to a chopping board. Turn over the aubergines and peppers and return them to the oven for a further 20 minutes.

2 Meanwhile, peel the garlic cloves and place them in a blender or food processor.

3 When the peppers are blistered and charred, use tongs to transfer them to a plastic bag, tie the top and leave to cool. Return the aubergines to the oven for a further 10 minutes.

4 Remove the aubergines from the oven. Split them in half and scoop the flesh into a sieve (strainer) placed over a bowl. Press the flesh with a spoon to remove the bitter juices.

5 Add the aubergine flesh to the garlic and process until smooth. Place in a large mixing bowl.

6 Peel and seed the red peppers and chop the flesh. Stir it into the aubergine mixture. Mix in the pink peppercorns and chopped fresh coriander and serve immediately on a bed of mixed salad leaves.

> **Cook's Tip**
> Serve the pâté with Melba toast, oatcakes, fingers of olive focaccia or mini pitta breads.

Red Pepper Watercress Parcels

The peppery watercress flavour contrasts delightfully with sweet red pepper in these crisp filo parcels.

Makes 8

3 red (bell) peppers
175g/6oz watercress or
　　rocket (arugula)
225g/8oz 1 cup ricotta cheese
50g/2oz/½ cup toasted,
　　chopped almonds
8 sheets filo pastry, thawed
　　if frozen
30ml/2 tbsp olive oil
salt and ground black pepper

1 Preheat the oven to 190°C/375°F/Gas 5 and preheat the grill (broiler). Place the red peppers on a baking sheet and grill (broil), turning occasionally with tongs, until blistered and charred. Use tongs to transfer to a plastic bag, tie the top and leave to cool.

2 When the peppers are cool enough to handle, peel and seed them. Pat dry with kitchen paper.

3 Place the peppers and watercress or rocket in a food processor and pulse until coarsely chopped. Spoon the mixture into a bowl. Stir in the ricotta and almonds and season to taste with salt and pepper.

4 Working with one sheet of filo pastry at a time and keeping the others covered, cut out two 18cm/7in and two 5cm/2in squares from each sheet. Brush one large square with a little olive oil and place a second large square at an angle of 45 degrees to form a star shape.

5 Place one of the smaller squares in the centre of the star shape, brush lightly with olive oil and top with the second small square.

6 Top with one-eighth of the red pepper mixture. Bring the edges together to form a purse shape and twist to seal. Place on a lightly greased baking sheet and cook for 25–30 minutes, until golden. Serve immediately.

Pâté Energy 51kcal/213kJ; Protein 2.2g; Carbohydrate 8.9g, of which sugars 8.4g; Fat 1g, of which saturates 0.2g; Cholesterol 0mg; Calcium 22mg; Fibre 4.4g; Sodium 7mg.
Parcels Energy 163kcal/677kJ; Protein 5.9g; Carbohydrate 10.9g, of which sugars 5.7g; Fat 10.9g, of which saturates 3.4g; Cholesterol 12mg; Calcium 67mg; Fibre 2.1g; Sodium 15mg.

Nutty Cheese Balls

An extremely quick and simple recipe. Try making smaller portions to serve as canapés at a drinks party.

Serves 4

225g/8oz/1 cup low-fat soft (farmer's) cheese
50g/2oz/1/2 cup Dolcelatte or Gorgonzola cheese
15ml/1 tbsp finely chopped onion
15ml/1 tbsp finely chopped celery
15ml/1 tbsp finely chopped fresh parsley

15ml/1 tbsp finely chopped gherkin
5ml/1 tsp brandy or port (optional)
pinch of paprika
50g/2oz/1/2 cup walnuts, coarsely chopped
90ml/6 tbsp chopped fresh chives
salt and ground black pepper

To serve

crusty bread
mixed salad leaves
sliced radishes

1 Put the soft cheese and Dolcelatte or Gorgonzola in a bowl and beat with a spoon until combined and quite smooth.

2 Add the onion, celery, parsley, gherkin, brandy or port, if using, paprika and walnuts, season with salt and pepper and stir well to combine.

3 Divide the mixture into 12 pieces and roll each piece into a ball between the palms of your hands.

4 Roll each ball gently in the chopped chives and place on a plate. Cover with clear film (plastic wrap) or foil, and chill in the refrigerator for about 1 hour. Serve with crusty bread, mixed salad leaves and sliced radishes.

> **Variation**
> For an alternative look, mix the chives with the rest of the ingredients in step 2 but omit the walnuts. Instead, chop the walnuts very finely and use to coat the cheese balls in step 4. For a larger number of guests make one batch of each type and serve a mixture of the two.

Fried Tomatoes with Herb Polenta

This recipe works well with green tomatoes freshly picked from the garden or greenhouse.

Serves 4

750ml/1¼ pints/3 cups vegetable stock or water
5ml/1 tsp salt

175g/6oz/1 cup polenta
25g/1oz/2 tbsp butter
75ml/5 tbsp chopped mixed fresh parsley, thyme, chives and basil, plus extra, to garnish
olive oil, for greasing and brushing
6 large plum or beefsteak tomatoes
salt and ground black pepper

1 Prepare the polenta in advance: place the stock or water in a heavy pan, with the salt, and bring to the boil. Lower the heat, slowly pour in the polenta and stir with a wooden spoon.

2 Stir the mixture constantly, using a figure-eight action, over a medium heat for 5 minutes, until the polenta begins to thicken and come away from the sides of the pan.

3 Remove from the heat and continue stirring for another minute or two. Stir in the butter, freshly chopped parsley, thyme, chives and basil, and season with black pepper.

4 Tip the mixture into a wide, greased tin (pan) or a glass or ceramic dish. Using a flexible spatula, spread the polenta mixture out evenly. Cover the surface closely with greaseproof (waxed) paper, then put it in a cool place until it has set completely and is cold.

5 Turn out the polenta on to a board and stamp out 8 rounds using a large biscuit or cookie cutter. Alternatively, you can cut the polenta into 8 squares with a knife. Brush with oil.

6 Heat a griddle pan and lightly brush it with oil. Cut the tomatoes in two, then brush them with oil and sprinkle with salt and pepper. Cook the tomato halves and polenta patties on the pan for 5 minutes, turning them once.

7 Serve garnished with fresh herbs.

Cheese Balls Energy 213kcal/883kJ; Protein 13.4g; Carbohydrate 4g, of which sugars 3.5g; Fat 16.9g, of which saturates 6g; Cholesterol 23mg; Calcium 170mg; Fibre 1.4g; Sodium 409mg.
Tomatoes Energy 215kcal/897kJ; Protein 5g; Carbohydrate 24.1g, of which sugars 3.1g; Fat 10.9g, of which saturates 1.5g; Cholesterol 48mg; Calcium 15mg; Fibre 1.6g; Sodium 27mg.

Bean Purée with Grilled Vegetables

The slightly bitter radicchio
and chicory make a
wonderful marriage with the
creamy citrus bean purée.

Serves 4
400g/14oz can cannellini beans
45ml/3 tbsp low-fat fromage
 blanc (farmer's cheese)

finely grated rind and juice of
 1 large orange
15ml/1 tbsp finely chopped
 fresh rosemary
4 heads of chicory
 (Belgian endive)
2 radicchio
15ml/1 tbsp walnut oil

1 Preheat the grill (broiler). Drain the beans, rinse, and drain
again. Put the beans, cheese, half the orange rind, the orange
juice and rosemary in a food processor or blender and process
until combined. Set aside.

2 Cut the heads of chicory in half lengthways. Cut each
radicchio into eight wedges.

3 Spread out the chicory and radicchio on a baking sheet and
brush with walnut oil. Grill (broil) for 2–3 minutes. Serve the
leaves with the bean purée, sprinkled with the remaining
orange rind.

Variations
• For a Middle Eastern flavour, substitute 30ml/2 tbsp tahini,
also known as sesame seed paste, for the orange juice and
omit the orange rind. Add 4 chopped spring onions (scallions) to
the mixture in the food processor or blender and substitute
chopped fresh mint for the rosemary. If the mixture seems too
thick, add 15ml/1 tbsp olive oil. Garnish with fresh mint sprigs.
• For a North African flavour, substitute canned broad (fava)
beans for the cannellini beans, 1½ lemons for the orange and
5ml/1 tsp ground cumin for the rosemary.
• For a Tex-Mex treat, substitute canned red kidney beans for
the cannellini beans, 2 limes for the orange and 2–3 seeded
and finely chopped fresh red chillies for the rosemary.

Broccoli & Chestnut Terrine

Served hot or cold, this
versatile terrine is just as
suitable for a dinner party
as for a picnic.

Serves 4–6
450g/1lb/4 cups broccoli florets
225g/8oz/2 cups cooked
 chestnuts, coarsely chopped
50g/2oz/1 cup fresh wholemeal
 (whole-wheat) breadcrumbs

60ml/4 tbsp low-fat natural
 (plain) yogurt
30ml/2 tbsp finely grated
 Parmesan cheese
pinch of freshly grated nutmeg
2 eggs, lightly beaten
salt and ground black pepper
boiled new potatoes and mixed
 salad leaves, to serve

1 Preheat the oven to 180°C/350°F/Gas 4. Base-line a 900g/2lb
non-stick loaf tin (pan) with baking parchment.

2 Blanch or steam the broccoli for 3–4 minutes, until just
tender. Drain well. Reserve a quarter of the smallest florets and
chop the rest finely.

3 Mix together the chestnuts, breadcrumbs, yogurt, Parmesan
and nutmeg and season to taste with salt and pepper. Fold in
the chopped broccoli, reserved florets and the beaten eggs.

4 Spoon the broccoli mixture into the prepared tin. Place in a
roasting pan and pour in boiling water to come about halfway
up the sides of the loaf tin. Bake for 20–25 minutes.

5 Remove the terrine from the oven and invert on to a
warmed plate or tray. Cut into even slices and serve
immediately with new potatoes and salad leaves. Alternatively,
leave the terrine in the loaf tin to cool completely, then turn
out and serve cold.

Cook's Tip
*If you do not have a non-stick loaf tin (pan), grease it lightly
with olive or sunflower oil after base-lining.*

Purée Energy 148kcal/623kJ; Protein 8.2g; Carbohydrate 19.6g, of which sugars 5.3g; Fat 4.6g, of which saturates 1.1g; Cholesterol 1mg; Calcium 105mg; Fibre 6.9g; Sodium 396mg.
Terrine Energy 169kcal/711kJ; Protein 9.4g; Carbohydrate 22g, of which sugars 4.5g; Fat 5.4g, of which saturates 1.9g; Cholesterol 69mg; Calcium 152mg; Fibre 3.7g; Sodium 157mg.

Baked Squash with Parmesan

Spaghetti squash is an unusual vegetable – when baked, the flesh separates into long strands.

Serves 2

1 spaghetti squash
115g/4oz/½ cup butter
45ml/3 tbsp mixed chopped fresh
   herbs such as parsley, chives
   and oregano
1 garlic clove, crushed
1 shallot, chopped
5ml/1 tsp lemon juice
50g/2oz/⅔ cup freshly grated
   Parmesan cheese
salt and ground black pepper

1 Preheat the oven to 180°C/350°F/Gas 4. Cut the squash in half lengthways. Place the halves, cut-sides down, in a roasting pan. Pour a little water around them, then bake for about 40 minutes, until tender.

2 Meanwhile, put the butter, herbs, garlic, shallot and lemon juice in a food processor or blender and process until thoroughly blended and creamy in consistency. Season to taste with salt and pepper.

3 When the squash is tender, scrape out and discard any seeds, then cut a thin slice from the base of each half, so that they will sit level. Place the squash halves on warmed serving plates.

4 Using a fork, pull out a few of the spaghetti-like strands in the centre of each. Add a spoonful of herb butter, then sprinkle with a little of the grated Parmesan. Serve the remaining herb butter and Parmesan separately, adding them as you pull out more strands.

Cook's Tip
Spaghetti squash is also good served with simple garlic butter. If you don't want to bother making a herb butter of any sort, serve with a dish of ready-made pesto.

Asparagus Rolls with Herb Sauce

For a taste sensation, try tender asparagus spears wrapped in crisp filo pastry served with a rich, buttery herb sauce.

Serves 2

50g/2oz/¼ cup butter, plus extra
   for greasing
5 sheets filo pastry
10 asparagus spears
salad, to garnish (optional)

For the sauce

2 shallots, finely chopped
1 bay leaf
150ml/¼ pint/⅔ cup dry
   white wine
175g/6oz/¾ cup butter, softened
15ml/1 tbsp chopped fresh
   herbs, such as parsley, basil
   and thyme
salt and ground black pepper
chopped fresh chives, to garnish

1 Preheat the oven to 200°C/400°F/Gas 6. Grease a baking sheet. Melt the ¼ cup butter. Cut the filo pastry sheets in half. Brush a half sheet with melted butter. Fold one corner of the sheet down to the bottom edge to give a wedge shape.

2 Trim the asparagus, then lay a spear on top at the longest pastry edge and roll up towards the shortest edge. Make nine more rolls in the same way.

3 Lay the rolls on the prepared baking sheet. Brush with the remaining melted butter. Bake in the preheated oven for about 8 minutes, until golden.

4 Meanwhile, put the shallots, bay leaf and wine into a pan. Cover with a tight-fitting lid and cook over high heat until the wine is reduced to 45–60ml/3–4 tbsp.

5 Strain the wine mixture into a bowl. Whisk in the ¾ cup butter, a little at a time, until the sauce is smooth and glossy.

6 Stir in the herbs and season to taste with salt and pepper. Return to the pan and keep the sauce warm. Serve the asparagus rolls on warmed individual plates with a salad garnish, if you like. Sprinkle the butter sauce with a few chopped chives and hand around separately.

Squash Energy 597kcal/2467kJ; Protein 13g; Carbohydrate 10.4g, of which sugars 8g; Fat 56.2g, of which saturates 35.5g; Cholesterol 148mg; Calcium 420mg; Fibre 3.9g; Sodium 622mg.
Asparagus Energy 986kcal/4066kJ; Protein 5.1g; Carbohydrate 20.7g, of which sugars 4.6g; Fat 93.4g, of which saturates 58.7g; Cholesterol 240mg; Calcium 121mg; Fibre 3g; Sodium 694mg.

Multi-mushroom Stroganoff

A pan-fry of sliced mushrooms swirled with sour cream makes a delicious accompaniment to pasta or rice.

Serves 3–4

45ml/3 tbsp olive oil
450g/1lb fresh mixed wild and cultivated mushrooms such as ceps, shiitakes or oysters, sliced
3 spring onions (scallions), sliced
2 garlic cloves, crushed
30ml/2 tbsp dry sherry or vermouth
300ml/½ pint/1¼ cups sour cream or crème fraîche
15ml/1 tbsp chopped fresh marjoram or thyme leaves
chopped fresh chives, to garnish
rice, pasta or potatoes, to serve

1 Heat the oil in a large frying pan over low heat. Add the mushrooms and cook, stirring occasionally, for about 5 minutes, until they are softened and just cooked.

2 Add the spring onions, garlic and sherry or vermouth and cook for 1 minute more. Season well with salt and pepper.

3 Stir in the sour cream or crème fraîche and heat to just below boiling point. Stir in the marjoram or thyme, then sprinkle over the chopped chives. Serve with rice, pasta or boiled new potatoes.

Cook's Tips
• *To create the most interesting flavour in this dish, use at least three different varieties of mushroom, preferably incorporating some woodland or wild mushrooms.*
• *It is important not to let the mixture boil after adding the cream. Like single (light) cream, sour cream and crème fraîche have a tendency to curdle when heated even though they both contain slightly more butterfat (single cream 19 per cent, sour cream 20 per cent, crème fraîche 15–40 per cent). Curdling is also much more likely to occur if the other ingredients in the pan include something acidic, such as lemon juice or, as in this case, sherry or vermouth.*

Mushroom Flan

Mushrooms, baby corn and spinach make a delectable filling for a flan, especially when sunflower seeds are included.

Serves 6

175g/6oz/1½ cups wholemeal (whole-wheat) flour
75g/3oz/6 tbsp low-fat spread
45ml/3 tbsp olive oil
175g/6oz baby corn, each cut into 2–3 pieces
30ml/2 tbsp sunflower seeds
225g/8oz/2 cups mushrooms
75g/3oz fresh spinach leaves, chopped
juice of 1 lemon
sea salt and ground black pepper
tomato salad, to serve

1 Preheat the oven to 180°C/350°F/Gas 4. Sift the flour into a bowl, then add the bran from the sieve (strainer). Rub in the low-fat spread until the mixture resembles breadcrumbs. Add enough water to make a firm dough.

2 Roll out the dough on a lightly floured surface and line a 23cm/9in flan dish. Prick the base, line the flan case with foil and add a layer of baking beans. Bake blind for 15 minutes, then remove the foil and beans. Return the pastry case to the oven and bake for a further 10 minutes, or until the pastry is crisp and golden brown.

3 Meanwhile, heat the oil in a heavy-based pan. Fry the corn with the sunflower seeds for 5–8 minutes until lightly browned.

4 Add the button mushrooms, lower the heat slightly and cook the mixture for 2–3 minutes, then stir in the chopped spinach. Cover the pan and cook for 2–3 minutes.

5 Sharpen the filling with a little lemon juice. Stir in salt and pepper to taste. Spoon into the flan case. Serve warm or cold with a tomato salad.

Cook's Tip
If the mushrooms are small, leave them whole or cut into halves.

Stroganoff Energy 253kcal/1044kJ; Protein 4.4g; Carbohydrate 3.6g, of which sugars 3.4g; Fat 23.8g, of which saturates 10.7g; Cholesterol 45mg; Calcium 80mg; Fibre 1.4g; Sodium 38mg.
Mushroom Flan Energy 232kcal/970kJ; Protein 7.3g; Carbohydrate 20.6g, of which sugars 1.4g; Fat 14g, of which saturates 2.5g; Cholesterol 1mg; Calcium 47mg; Fibre 4g; Sodium 434mg.

Tofu & Crunchy Vegetables

High protein tofu is nicest if it is marinated lightly before it is cooked.

Serves 4

2 x 225g/8oz packets smoked tofu, diced
45ml/3 tbsp soy sauce
30ml/2 tbsp dry sherry or vermouth
15ml/1 tbsp sesame oil
45ml/3 tbsp groundnut (peanut) or sunflower oil
2 leeks, thinly sliced
2 carrots, cut into batons
1 large courgette (zucchini), thinly sliced
115g/4oz baby corn, halved
115g/4oz button (white) or shiitake mushrooms, sliced
15ml/1 tbsp sesame seeds
cooked noodles dressed with sesame oil, to serve (optional)

1 Place the tofu in a shallow dish. Mix together the soy sauce, sherry or vermouth and sesame oil and pour over the tofu. Cover with clear film (plastic wrap) and leave to marinate in a cool place for at least 30 minutes. Drain the tofu cubes and reserve the marinade.

2 Heat a wok or large, heavy frying pan and add the groundnut oil. When the oil is hot, add the tofu cubes and stir-fry until browned all over. Remove the tofu from the pan.

3 Add the leeks, carrots, courgette and baby corn to the pan and stir-fry for about 2 minutes. Add the mushrooms and cook for 1 minute more.

4 Return the tofu to the pan and pour in the reserved marinade. Heat, stirring gently, until bubbling, then sprinkle with the sesame seeds. Serve immediately with hot cooked noodles dressed with a little sesame oil, if you like.

> **Cook's Tip**
> *The actual cooking of this dish takes just a few minutes, so have all the ingredients prepared before you start.*

Sprouting Beans & Pak Choi

Stir-frying is a great way to cook vegetables as they retain their colour, texture and most of their nutrients.

Serves 4

45ml/3 tbsp groundnut (peanut) oil
3 spring onions (scallions), sliced
2 garlic cloves, cut into slivers
2.5cm/1in piece fresh root ginger, cut into slivers
1 carrot, cut into thick batons
150g/5oz/scant 1 cup sprouting beans (lentils, mung beans, chickpeas)
200g/7oz pak choi (bok choy), shredded
50g/2oz/½ cup unsalted cashew nuts or halved almonds

For the sauce

45ml/3 tbsp light soy sauce
30ml/2 tbsp dry sherry
15ml/1 tbsp sesame oil
150ml/¼ pint/⅔ cup cold water
5ml/1 tsp cornflour (cornstarch)
5ml/1 tsp clear honey
salt and ground black pepper

1 Heat a large wok and add the oil. When the oil is hot add the spring onions, garlic, ginger and carrot and stir-fry over medium heat for 2 minutes.

2 Add the sprouting beans and stir-fry for a further 2 minutes. Add the pak choi and cashew nuts or almonds and stir-fry until the leaves are just wilting.

3 Mix all the sauce ingredients together in a jug (pitcher) and pour into the wok, stirring constantly.

4 When all the vegetables are coated in a thin glossy sauce season with salt and pepper. Serve immediately.

> **Variation**
> *You can use a variety of other Chinese greens besides pak choi (bok choy). Try Chinese leaves (Chinese cabbage), Chinese flowering cabbage, Chinese spinach, also known as callaloo, or Chinese water spinach.*

Tofu Energy 251kcal/1040kJ; Protein 12.6g; Carbohydrate 7.2g, of which sugars 5.8g; Fat 18.3g, of which saturates 2.4g; Cholesterol 0mg; Calcium 578mg; Fibre 3.8g; Sodium 877mg.
Pak Choi Energy 230kcal/954kJ; Protein 5g; Carbohydrate 11.3g, of which sugars 7.6g; Fat 17.7g, of which saturates 3.3g; Cholesterol 0mg; Calcium 46mg; Fibre 2.4g; Sodium 848mg.

Tomato Omelette Envelopes

These delicious chive omelettes are folded and filled with tomato and melting Camembert cheese.

Serves 2

1 small onion
4 tomatoes
30ml/2 tbsp vegetable oil

4 eggs
30ml/2 tbsp chopped fresh chives
115g/4oz Camembert cheese, rinded and diced
salt and ground black pepper
lettuce leaves and Granary (whole-wheat) bread, to serve (optional)

1 Cut the onion in half and cut each half into thin wedges. Cut the tomatoes into wedges of similar size.

2 Heat 15ml/1 tbsp of the oil in a frying pan. Add the onion and cook over medium heat for 2 minutes. Increase the heat, add the tomatoes and cook for a further 2 minutes, then remove the pan from the heat.

3 Beat the eggs with the chives in a bowl and season with salt and pepper. Heat the remaining oil in an omelette pan. Add half the egg mixture and tilt the pan to spread thinly. Cook for 1 minute. Flip the omelette over and cook for 1 minute more. Remove from the pan and keep hot. Make a second omelette with the remaining egg mixture.

4 Return the tomato mixture to high heat. Add the cheese and toss the mixture over the heat for 1 minute.

5 Divide the mixture between the omelettes and fold them over. Serve immediately with crisp lettuce leaves and chunks of Granary bread, if you like.

> **Variation**
> Add 2–3 sliced mushrooms to the tomato-onion filling. For a mushroom omelette, substitute 6–8 button (white) mushrooms for the tomato. They will need a slightly longer cooking time.

Curried Eggs

Hard-boiled eggs are served on a mild creamy sauce with just a hint of curry.

Serves 2

4 eggs
15ml/1 tbsp sunflower oil
1 small onion, chopped
2.5cm/1in piece of fresh root ginger, grated
2.5ml/½ tsp ground cumin
2.5ml/½ tsp garam masala

22.5ml/1½ tbsp tomato purée (paste)
10ml/2 tsp tandoori paste
10ml/2 tsp freshly squeezed lemon juice
50ml/2fl oz/¼ cup single (light) cream
15ml/1 tbsp finely chopped fresh coriander (cilantro)
salt and ground black pepper
fresh coriander sprigs, to garnish

1 Put the eggs in a pan of water. Bring to the boil, lower the heat and simmer for 10 minutes.

2 Meanwhile, heat the oil in a frying pan over medium heat. Add the onion and cook, stirring occasionally, for 2–3 minutes. Add the ginger and cook, stirring constantly, for 1 minute more.

3 Stir in the ground cumin, garam masala, tomato purée, tandoori paste, lemon juice and cream. Cook for 1–2 minutes more, but do not allow the mixture to boil. Stir in the chopped coriander and season to taste with salt and pepper.

4 Drain the eggs, remove the shells and cut each egg in half. Spoon the sauce into a serving bowl, top with the eggs and garnish with fresh coriander. Serve immediately.

> **Cook's Tip**
> It is recommended that you store eggs in the refrigerator for health reasons. Do not wash them, but equally do not use dirty eggs. Store eggs pointed ends downwards, and remove from the refrigerator about 30 minutes before you want to cook them to allow them to come to room temperature. This will help prevent them from cracking.

Omelette Energy 488kcal/2027kJ; Protein 26g; Carbohydrate 8.6g, of which sugars 7.9g; Fat 38.2g, of which saturates 15.1g; Cholesterol 434mg; Calcium 226mg; Fibre 2.4g; Sodium 479mg.
Curried Eggs Energy 310kcal/1286kJ; Protein 14.6g; Carbohydrate 2.7g, of which sugars 2.6g; Fat 27.2g, of which saturates 7.5g; Cholesterol 394mg; Calcium 133mg; Fibre 1.6g; Sodium 180mg.

Greek Spinach & Cheese Pies

These individual spinach, feta and Parmesan cheese pies are easy to make using ready-made filo pastry.

Makes 4

15ml/1 tbsp olive oil
1 small onion, finely chopped
275g/10oz/2½ cups spinach, stalks removed
50g/2oz/4 tbsp butter, melted
4 sheets filo pastry
1 egg
large pinch of freshly grated nutmeg
75g/3oz/¾ cup crumbled feta cheese
15ml/1 tbsp freshly grated Parmesan cheese
salt and ground black pepper

1 Preheat the oven to 190°C/375°F/Gas 5. Heat the oil in a large pan over low heat. Add the onion and cook, stirring occasionally, for 5–6 minutes, until softened. Add the spinach leaves and cook, stirring, until the spinach has wilted and most of the liquid has evaporated. Remove from the heat and leave to cool completely.

2 Brush four 10cm/4in diameter loose-based tartlet tins (muffin pans) with melted butter. Cut two sheets of filo into eight 14cm/4½in squares each.

3 Brush four squares at a time with melted butter. Line the first tartlet tin with one square, gently easing it into the base and up the sides. Leave the edges overhanging. Lay the remaining squares on top of the first, turning them so the corners form a star shape. Repeat for the remaining tins.

4 Beat the egg with the nutmeg and seasoning, then stir in the cheeses and spinach. Divide the mixture among the tins and smooth level. Fold the overhanging pastry over the filling.

5 Cut the third pastry sheet into eight 10cm/4in rounds. Brush with butter and place two on top of each tartlet. Press around the edges to seal. Brush the last pastry sheet with butter and cut into strips. Gently twist each strip and lay them on top of the tartlets. Bake for 30–35 minutes, until golden brown. Serve the pies hot or cold.

Potatoes with Blue Cheese

So often served as a mere accompaniment, potatoes also make a satisfying main dish, as here.

Serves 4

450g/1lb small new potatoes
small head of celery, sliced
small red onion, thinly sliced
115g/4oz blue cheese, mashed
150ml/¼ pint/⅔ cup single (light) cream
90g/3½ oz/scant 1 cup walnut pieces
30ml/2 tbsp chopped fresh parsley
salt and ground black pepper

1 Put the potatoes in a pan, add water to cover and bring to the boil. Cook for about 15 minutes, adding the sliced celery and onion to the pan for the last 5 minutes or so.

2 Drain the vegetables well and put them into a warmed, shallow serving dish, making sure that they are evenly distributed. Keep warm.

3 Put the cheese and cream in a small pan and melt over low heat, stirring frequently. Do not allow the mixture to boil, but heat it until it scalds.

4 Season the sauce to taste with salt and pepper, bearing in mind that the cheese will already be quite salty. Pour it over the vegetables and sprinkle the walnuts and chopped parsley over the top. Serve immediately.

> **Cook's Tip**
> Choose any blue cheese you like, such as Stilton, Danish blue, Blue Vinney or blue Brie.

> **Variation**
> Substitute a thinly sliced fennel bulb for the celery if you like its distinctive aniseed-like flavour.

Potatoes Energy 419kcal/1744kJ; Protein 13.3g; Carbohydrate 22g, of which sugars 4.8g; Fat 31.6g, of which saturates 11.4g; Cholesterol 42mg; Calcium 261mg; Fibre 3.6g; Sodium 439mg.
Cheese Pies Energy 287kcal/1191kJ; Protein 9.9g; Carbohydrate 17.2g, of which sugars 2.5g; Fat 20.3g, of which saturates 10.7g; Cholesterol 91mg; Calcium 269mg; Fibre 2.2g; Sodium 502mg.

Chilli Beans with Basmati Rice

Red kidney beans, chopped tomatoes and hot chilli make a great combination in this colourful dish.

Serves 4
350g/12oz/2 cups basmati rice
30ml/2 tbsp olive oil
1 large onion, chopped
1 garlic clove, crushed
15ml/12 tbsp hot chilli powder
15g/¹/₂oz/2 tbsp plain (all-
    purpose) flour
15ml/1 tbsp tomato
    purée (paste)
400g/14oz can
    chopped tomatoes
400g/14oz can red kidney
    beans, drained
150ml/¹/₄ pint/²/₃ cup hot
    vegetable stock
salt and ground black pepper
chopped fresh parsley, to garnish

1 Wash the rice several times under cold running water. Drain well. Bring a large pan of water to the boil. Add the rice and cook for 10–12 minutes, until tender. Meanwhile, heat the oil in a frying pan over low heat. Add the onion and garlic and cook, stirring occasionally, for about 2 minutes.

2 Stir the chilli powder and flour into the onion and garlic mixture and cook, stirring frequently, for 2 minutes more.

3 Stir in the tomato purée and chopped tomatoes. Rinse and drain the kidney beans well and add to the pan with the hot vegetable stock. Cover and simmer gently, stirring occasionally, for 12 minutes.

4 Season the chilli sauce to taste with salt and pepper. Drain the rice and serve immediately with the chilli beans, garnished with a little chopped fresh parsley.

> **Cook's Tip**
> You can also serve the chilli beans with pasta, such as penne or conchiglie, or with hot pitta bread. They also make a really scrumptious filling for baked potatoes.

Lentil Stir-fry

Mushrooms, artichoke hearts, sugar snap peas and green lentils make a satisfying stir-fry supper.

Serves 2–3
115g/4oz/1 cup sugar snap peas
25g/1oz/2 tbsp butter
1 small onion, chopped
115g/4oz cup brown cap
  (cremini) mushrooms, sliced
400g/14oz can artichoke hearts,
    drained and halved
400g/14oz can green lentils,
    drained and rinsed
60ml/4 tbsp single (light) cream
25g/1oz/¹/₄ cup flaked (sliced)
    almonds, toasted
salt and ground black pepper
French bread, to serve

1 Bring a pan of salted water to the boil, add the sugar snap peas and cook for about 4 minutes, until just tender. Drain, refresh under cold running water, then drain again. Pat the peas dry with kitchen paper and set aside.

2 Melt the butter in a frying pan. Add the onion and cook over medium heat, stirring occasionally, for 2–3 minutes.

3 Add the mushrooms to the pan. Stir until well combined, then cook for 2–3 minutes, until just tender.

4 Add the artichoke hearts, sugar snap peas and lentils to the pan and cook, stirring constantly, for 2 minutes.

5 Stir in the cream and almonds and cook for 1 minute, but do not allow the mixture to come to the boil. Season to taste with salt and pepper. Spoon the stir-fry on to warmed plates and serve immediately with chunks of French bread.

> **Cook's Tip**
> Use dried green lentils if you prefer. Cook them in a pan of boiling water for 30–45 minutes first (without adding any salt), then drain well and add them to the stir-fry with the artichokes and sugar snap peas.

Chilli Beans Energy 523kcal/2194kJ; Protein 15.5g; Carbohydrate 100.1g, of which sugars 11.5g; Fat 7.1g, of which saturates 1g; Cholesterol 0mg; Calcium 120mg; Fibre 8.5g; Sodium 410mg.
Lentil Energy 345kcal/1443kJ; Protein 18.4g; Carbohydrate 30.9g, of which sugars 4.7g; Fat 17.3g, of which saturates 7.4g; Cholesterol 29mg; Calcium 139mg; Fibre 9.7g; Sodium 144mg.

Arabian Spinach

Stir-fry spinach with onions and spices, then mix in a can of chickpeas and you have a quick, delicious main meal.

Serves 4

30ml/2 tbsp olive or sunflower oil
1 onion, sliced
2 garlic cloves, crushed
5ml/1 tsp cumin seeds
400g/14oz/3½ cups spinach, washed and shredded
425g/15oz can chickpeas, drained and rinsed
knob (pat) of butter
salt and ground black pepper

1 Heat the oil in a large frying pan or wok over low heat. Add the onion and cook, stirring occasionally, for about 5 minutes, until softened but not coloured. Add the garlic and cumin seeds and cook, stirring constantly, for another minute.

2 Add the spinach, in batches, stirring until the leaves begin to wilt. Fresh spinach leaves collapse down dramatically on cooking and they will all fit into the pan.

3 Stir in the chickpeas and butter and season to taste with salt and pepper. Reheat until just bubbling, then serve immediately. Drain off any pan juices, if you like, but this dish is rather good served with a little sauce.

Cook's Tip
Always use spinach within a day of purchase as it does not keep well and quickly becomes slimy. Store it in a cool place and wash thoroughly and spin dry before cooking.

Variations
• *You can use other canned pulses (legumes) besides chickpeas for this dish. Ful medames, for example, would be a good choice, as their nutty flavour goes particularly well with cumin.*
• *For a more substantial dish, top with hot, quartered hard-boiled eggs.*

Courgettes en Papillote

An impressive dinner party side dish, these puffed paper parcels should be broken open at the table.

Serves 4

2 courgettes (zucchini)
1 leek
225g/8oz young asparagus, trimmed
4 fresh tarragon sprigs
4 garlic cloves, unpeeled
1 egg, beaten
salt and ground black pepper

1 Preheat the oven to 200°C/400°F/Gas 6. Using a vegetable peeler, slice the courgettes lengthways into thin strips.

2 Cut the leek into very fine julienne strips and cut the asparagus evenly into 5cm/2in lengths.

3 Cut out four sheets of greaseproof (waxed) paper measuring about 30 x 38cm/12 x 15in and fold in half. Draw a large curve to make a heart shape when unfolded. Cut along the inside of the line and open out.

4 Divide the courgettes, leek and asparagus evenly among each paper heart, positioning the filling on one side of the fold line, and topping each with a sprig of fresh tarragon and an unpeeled garlic clove. Season to taste with salt and pepper.

5 Brush the edges lightly with the beaten egg and fold over. Pleat the edges together so that each parcel is completely sealed. Lay the parcels on a baking sheet and bake for about 10 minutes. Serve immediately.

Variation
Experiment with other combinations of vegetables and herbs such as sugar snap peas or mangetouts (snow peas) and mint; baby carrots and rosemary; fine green beans or baby broad (fava) beans and savory; asparagus and basil – the possibilities are almost endless. Always include a member of the onion family, preferably one with a mild flavour.

Spinach Energy 201kcal/841kJ; Protein 11.4g; Carbohydrate 21g, of which sugars 3.4g; Fat 8.4g, of which saturates 1g; Cholesterol 0mg; Calcium 220mg; Fibre 6.6g; Sodium 146mg.
Courgettes Energy 60kcal/249kJ; Protein 5.7g; Carbohydrate 4.2g, of which sugars 3.7g; Fat 2.4g, of which saturates 0.6g; Cholesterol 48mg; Calcium 58mg; Fibre 2.8g; Sodium 20mg.

Green Lentil & Cabbage Salad

This warm crunchy salad makes a satisfying meal if served with crusty French bread or wholemeal rolls.

Serves 4–6
225g/8oz/1 cup Puy lentils
1.3 litres/2¼ pints/6 cups cold
  water
3 garlic cloves
1 bay leaf
1 small onion, peeled and studded
  with 2 cloves
15ml/1 tbsp olive oil
1 red onion, thinly sliced
15ml/1 tbsp fresh thyme leaves
350g/12oz/3 cups finely
  shredded cabbage
finely grated rind and juice of
  1 lemon
15ml/1 tbsp raspberry vinegar
salt and ground black pepper

1 Rinse the lentils in cold water and place in a large pan with the water, 1 peeled garlic clove, bay leaf and clove-studded onion. Bring to the boil and cook for about 10 minutes. Reduce the heat, cover the pan with a tight-fitting lid and simmer gently for 15–20 minutes. Drain well. Remove and discard the onion, garlic and bay leaf.

2 Heat the oil in a large pan over low heat. Add the red onion, 2 crushed garlic cloves and thyme and cook, stirring occasionally, for 5 minutes, until the onion has softened.

3 Add the shredded cabbage and cook, stirring occasionally, for 3–5 minutes, until just cooked but still crunchy.

4 Stir in the cooked lentils, grated lemon rind and juice and the raspberry vinegar. Season with salt and pepper to taste and serve immediately.

> **Variation**
> This recipe works equally well with other types of cabbage. Choose whatever is in season: white cabbage or Savoy, or try fresh spring greens (collards) instead.

Tomato & Basil Tart

You could make individual tartlets instead of one large tart if you prefer, but reduce the baking time slightly.

Serves 6–8
175g/6oz/1½ cups plain (all-
  purpose) flour
2.5ml/½ tsp salt
115g/4oz/½ cup butter or
  margarine, chilled
45–75ml/3–5 tbsp water
salt and ground black pepper

For the filling
30ml/2 tbsp extra virgin olive oil
175g/6oz mozzarella cheese,
  thinly sliced
12 fresh basil leaves,
  6 coarsely torn
4–5 tomatoes, cut into
  5mm/¼in slices
60ml/4 tbsp freshly grated
  Parmesan cheese

1 Sift the flour and salt into a bowl, then rub in the butter until the mixture resembles breadcrumbs. Add 45ml/3 tbsp water and combine with a fork until the dough holds together. Mix in more water if necessary. Gather the dough into a ball, wrap in baking parchment and chill in the refrigerator for 40 minutes. Preheat the oven to 190°C/375°F/Gas 5.

2 Roll out the dough to a thickness of 5mm/¼in and use to line a 28cm/11in fluted loose-based flan tin (pan). Prick the base all over and chill in the refrigerator for 20 minutes.

3 Line the pastry case (pie shell) with a sheet of baking parchment and fill with dried beans. Place the flan tin on a baking sheet and bake blind for 15 minutes. Remove from the oven but leave the oven switched on.

4 Remove the beans and paper. Brush the pastry case with oil. Line with the mozzarella. Sprinkle the torn basil over the top.

5 Arrange the tomato slices over the cheese. Dot with the whole basil leaves. Season with salt and pepper, and sprinkle with Parmesan and oil. Bake for 35 minutes. If the cheese exudes a lot of liquid during baking, tilt the tin and spoon it off to keep the crust crisp. Serve hot or at room temperature.

Salad Energy 151kcal/638kJ; Protein 10.2g; Carbohydrate 22.8g, of which sugars 4.4g; Fat 2.7g, of which saturates 0.3g; Cholesterol 0mg; Calcium 60mg; Fibre 4.9g; Sodium 9mg.
Tart Energy 307kcal/1279kJ; Protein 9.6g; Carbohydrate 19g, of which sugars 2.4g; Fat 21.9g, of which saturates 12.5g; Cholesterol 51mg; Calcium 207mg; Fibre 1.3g; Sodium 262mg.

Spinach & Potato Galette

Creamy layers of potato, spinach and fresh herbs make a warming and filling supper dish.

Serves 6
900g/2lb large potatoes
450g/1lb/4 cups spinach
400g/14oz/1¾ cups low-fat cream cheese
15ml/1 tbsp wholegrain mustard
2 eggs
50g/2oz mixed chopped fresh herbs, such as chives, parsley, chervil or sorrel
salt and ground black pepper

1 Preheat the oven to 180°C/350°F/Gas 4. Base-line a deep 23cm/9in round cake tin (pan) with baking parchment.

2 Place the potatoes in a large pan and add cold water to cover. Bring to the boil, cover and cook for 10 minutes. Drain well and leave to cool slightly before slicing thinly.

3 Wash the spinach and place in another large pan with only the water that is clinging to the leaves. Cover and cook, stirring once, until the spinach has just wilted. Drain well in a sieve (strainer) and squeeze out the excess moisture with the back of a spoon. Chop the spinach finely.

4 Beat together the cream cheese, mustard and eggs in a bowl, then stir in the chopped spinach and fresh herbs.

5 Place a layer of the sliced potatoes in the lined tin, arranging them in concentric circles. Top with a spoonful of the cream cheese mixture and spread out. Continue layering, seasoning with salt and pepper as you go, until all the potatoes and the cream cheese mixture are used up.

6 Cover the tin with a piece of foil, scrunched around the edge, and place in a roasting pan.

7 Pour boiling water into the roasting pan to come about halfway up the sides and cook the galette in the oven for 45–50 minutes. Turn out on to a plate and serve immediately or leave to cool completely and serve cold.

Cowboy Hot-pot

A great dish to serve as a children's main meal, which adults will enjoy too – if they are allowed to join the posse.

Serves 4–6
45ml/3 tbsp sunflower oil
1 onion, sliced
1 red (bell) pepper, seeded and sliced
1 sweet potato or 2 carrots, chopped
115g/4oz/scant ½ cup chopped green beans
400g/14oz can baked beans
200g/7oz can corn
15ml/1 tbsp tomato purée (paste)
5ml/1 tsp barbecue spice seasoning
115g/4oz cheese (preferably smoked), diced
450g/1lb potatoes, thinly sliced
25g/1oz/2 tbsp butter, melted
salt and ground black pepper

1 Preheat the oven to 190°C/375°F/Gas 5. Heat the oil in a frying pan over low heat. Add the onion, red pepper and sweet potato or carrots and cook, stirring occasionally, for about 5 minutes, until softened but not coloured.

2 Increase the heat to medium and stir in the green beans, baked beans, corn (and liquid), tomato purée and barbecue spice seasoning. Bring to the boil, then lower the heat and simmer for 5 minutes.

3 Transfer the vegetable mixture to an ovenproof dish and stir in the diced cheese.

4 Cover the vegetable and cheese mixture with the potato slices, brush generously with the melted butter and season with salt and pepper. Bake the hot-pot for 30–40 minutes, until golden brown on top and the potato is cooked. Serve immediately straight from the dish.

Cook's Tip
Use any vegetable mixture you like in this versatile hot-pot, depending on what you have to hand.

Galette Energy 239kcal/1004kJ; Protein 16.9g; Carbohydrate 27.9g, of which sugars 5.6g; Fat 8.4g, of which saturates 4.2g; Cholesterol 79mg; Calcium 240mg; Fibre 3.5g; Sodium 440mg.
Hot-pot Energy 351kcal/1470kJ; Protein 12g; Carbohydrate 40.1g, of which sugars 11.1g; Fat 16.6g, of which saturates 7.3g; Cholesterol 27mg; Calcium 199mg; Fibre 5.7g; Sodium 503mg.

Quorn with Ginger, Chilli & Leeks

Quorn easily absorbs different flavours and retains a good firm texture, making it ideal for stir-frying.

Serves 4
225g/8oz packet Quorn, diced
45ml/3 tbsp dark soy sauce
30ml/2 tbsp dry sherry
  or vermouth
10ml/2 tsp clear honey
150ml/¼ pint/⅔ cup vegetable
  stock
10ml/2 tsp cornflour (cornstarch)
45ml/3 tbsp sunflower or
  groundnut (peanut) oil
3 leeks, thinly sliced
1 red chilli, seeded and sliced
2.5cm/1in piece fresh root
  ginger, shredded
salt and ground black pepper
rice or egg noodles, to serve

1 Toss the Quorn in the soy sauce and sherry or vermouth in a bowl until well coated. Leave to marinate for 30 minutes.

2 Drain the Quorn and reserve the marinade in a jug (pitcher). Mix the marinade with the honey, vegetable stock and cornflour to make a paste.

3 Heat the oil in a wok or large frying pan and, when hot, add the Quorn and stir-fry until it is crisp on the outside. Remove the Quorn and set aside.

4 Reheat the oil. Add the leeks, chilli and ginger and stir-fry for about 2 minutes, until they are just soft. Season to taste with salt and pepper.

5 Return the Quorn to the pan, together with the marinade mixture, and stir well until the liquid is thick and glossy. Serve immediately with rice or egg noodles.

Cook's Tip
Quorn is a versatile, mycoprotein food, now available in most supermarkets. If you cannot find it, you could use tofu instead.

Chinese Potatoes with Chilli Beans

This Chinese-inspired dish is made particularly appealing by its tasty sauce.

Serves 4
4 potatoes, cut into thick chunks
30ml/2 tbsp sunflower or
  groundnut (peanut) oil
3 spring onions (scallions), sliced
1 large chilli, seeded and sliced
2 garlic cloves, crushed
400g/14oz can red kidney
  beans, drained
30ml/2 tbsp dark soy sauce
15ml/1 tbsp sesame oil
salt and ground black pepper
15ml/1 tbsp sesame seeds,
  to sprinkle
chopped fresh coriander (cilantro)
  or parsley, to garnish

1 Put the potatoes in a pan, add cold water to cover and bring to the boil. Cover and cook for about 15 minutes, until they are just tender but still firm. Take care not to overcook them. Drain well and set aside.

2 Heat the oil in a wok or large, heavy frying pan. Add the spring onions and chilli and stir-fry over a medium heat for about 1 minute, then add the garlic and stir-fry for a few seconds longer.

3 Rinse and drain the kidney beans, then add them to the pan with the potatoes, stirring well. Finally, stir in the soy sauce and sesame oil.

4 Season to taste with salt and pepper and cook the vegetables until they are well heated through. Sprinkle with the sesame seeds and serve immediately, garnished with the chopped fresh coriander or parsley.

Cook's Tip
Coriander (cilantro) is also known as Chinese parsley and Greek parsley and it does resemble flat leaf parsley in appearance. However, the flavour is quite different. It is intensely aromatic, almost spicy, and goes especially well with chillies. It is one of those herbs that you either love or loathe.

Quorn Energy 158kcal/657kJ; Protein 8.6g; Carbohydrate 5.1g, of which sugars 3.8g; Fat 10.6g, of which saturates 1.4g; Cholesterol 0mg; Calcium 27mg; Fibre 4.9g; Sodium 939mg.
Potatoes Energy 272kcal/1141kJ; Protein 9.7g; Carbohydrate 34.8g, of which sugars 5.7g; Fat 11.4g, of which saturates 1.6g; Cholesterol 0mg; Calcium 107mg; Fibre 7.6g; Sodium 936mg.

Corn & Bean Tamale Pie

This hearty dish has a cheese-flavoured polenta topping which covers corn and kidney beans in a rich hot sauce. It is substantial enough for meat-eaters.

Serves 4

2 corn on the cob
30ml/2 tbsp vegetable oil
1 onion, chopped
2 garlic cloves, crushed
1 red (bell) pepper, seeded
  and chopped
2 green chillies, seeded
  and chopped
10ml/2 tbsp ground cumin
450g/1lb ripe tomatoes, peeled,
  seeded and chopped
15ml/1 tbsp tomato purée
  (paste)
425g/15oz can red kidney beans,
  drained and rinsed
15ml/1 tbsp chopped
  fresh oregano
oregano leaves, to garnish

For the topping

115g/4oz/scant 1 cup polenta
15g/½oz/2 tbsp plain (all-
  purpose) flour
2.5ml/½ tsp salt
10ml/2 tsp baking powder
1 egg, lightly beaten
120ml/4fl oz/½ cup milk
15g/½oz/1 tbsp butter, melted
50g/2oz/½ cup grated smoked
  Cheddar cheese

1 Preheat the oven to 220°C/425°F/Gas 7. Husk the corn on the cob, then par-boil for 8 minutes. Drain well, leave to cool slightly, then remove the kernels with a sharp knife.

2 Heat the oil in a large pan. Add the onion, garlic and red pepper and cook over low heat, stirring occasionally, for about 5 minutes, until softened. Add the chillies and cumin and cook, stirring constantly, for 1 minute. Stir in the tomatoes, tomato purée, beans, corn kernels and oregano. Season with salt and pepper. Simmer, uncovered, for 10 minutes.

3 To make the topping, mix the polenta, flour, salt, baking powder, egg, milk and butter to form a thick batter.

4 Transfer the bean mixture to an ovenproof dish, spoon the polenta mixture over and spread evenly. Bake for 30 minutes. Remove from the oven, sprinkle the cheese over the top, then bake for a further 5–10 minutes, until golden.

Pepper & Potato Tortilla

A traditional Spanish dish, tortilla is best eaten cold in chunky wedges and makes an ideal picnic food.

Serves 4

2 potatoes
45ml/3 tbsp olive oil
1 large onion, thinly sliced
2 garlic cloves, crushed
1 green (bell) pepper, seeded and
  thinly sliced
1 red (bell) pepper, seeded and
  thinly sliced
6 eggs, beaten
115g/4oz/1 cup grated
  mature (sharp) Cheddar or
  Mahón cheese
salt and ground black pepper

1 Do not peel the potatoes, but scrub them well under cold running water. Par-boil them for about 10 minutes, then drain and, when they are cool enough to handle, slice them thickly. Preheat the grill (broiler).

2 Heat the oil in a large non-stick or well seasoned frying pan. Add the onion, garlic and green and red peppers and cook over medium heat, stirring occasionally, for about 5 minutes, until softened but not coloured.

3 Add the potatoes, lower the heat and cook, stirring occasionally, until the potatoes are completely cooked and the vegetables are soft. Add a little extra olive oil if the pan seems too dry.

4 Pour in half the beaten eggs, then sprinkle over half the grated cheese. Add the rest of the eggs. Season with salt and pepper and sprinkle with the remaining cheese.

5 Continue to cook over low heat, without stirring, half covering the pan with a lid to help set the eggs.

6 When the mixture is firm, place the pan under the hot grill for a few seconds to seal the top lightly. Leave the tortilla in the pan to cool. This helps it firm up further and makes it easier to turn out. Cut into generous wedges or squares and serve at room temperature.

Pie Energy 513kcal/2154kJ; Protein 19.5g; Carbohydrate 71.1g, of which sugars 19.8g; Fat 17.6g, of which saturates 6.4g; Cholesterol 69mg; Calcium 233mg; Fibre 10.2g; Sodium 758mg.
Tortilla Energy 321kcal/1333kJ; Protein 13.1g; Carbohydrate 19.6g, of which sugars 10.2g; Fat 21.1g, of which saturates 8.3g; Cholesterol 123mg; Calcium 256mg; Fibre 3g; Sodium 254mg.

Potato & Broccoli Stir-fry

This wonderful stir-fry combines potato, broccoli and red pepper with just a hint of fresh ginger.

Serves 2
450g/1lb potatoes
45ml/3 tbsp groundnut (peanut) oil

50g/2oz/4 tbsp butter
1 small onion, chopped
1 red (bell) pepper, seeded and chopped
225g/8oz broccoli, broken into florets
2.5cm/1in piece of fresh root ginger, grated
salt and ground black pepper

1 Peel the potatoes and cut them into 1cm/½in dice. Heat the oil in a large frying pan. Add the potatoes and cook over a high heat, stirring and tossing frequently, for about 8 minutes, until browned and just tender.

2 Drain off the oil from the pan. Add the butter to the potatoes in the pan. As soon as it melts, add the onion and red pepper and stir-fry for 2 minutes.

3 Add the broccoli florets and ginger to the pan. Stir-fry for a further 2–3 minutes, taking care not to break up the potatoes. Season to taste with salt and pepper and serve immediately.

Cook's Tip
Always use a vegetable peeler with a swivel blade for peeling potatoes. As most of the nutrients are directly beneath the skin, it is important to peel them as thinly as possible.

Variations
• Substitute 1 finely chopped celery stick and 1 thinly sliced carrot for the red (bell) pepper.
• For a milder tasting dish, omit the ginger, replace the broccoli with peeled, seeded and diced tomatoes and flavour with torn fresh basil leaves.

Chickpea Stew

This hearty chickpea and vegetable stew is delicious served with garlic-flavoured mashed potato.

Serves 4
30ml/2 tbsp olive oil
1 small onion, finely chopped
225g/8oz carrots, halved lengthways and thinly sliced
2.5ml/½ tsp ground cumin
5ml/1 tsp ground coriander

25g/1oz/¼ cup plain (all-purpose) flour
225g/8oz courgettes (zucchini), sliced
200g/7oz can corn, drained
400g/14oz can chickpeas, drained and rinsed
30ml/2 tbsp tomato purée (paste)
200ml/7fl oz/scant 1 cup hot vegetable stock
salt and ground black pepper
mashed potato, to serve

1 Heat the olive oil in a frying pan. Add the onion and carrots and cook over medium heat, stirring occasionally, for about 5 minutes, until the onion has softened but not coloured.

2 Add the ground cumin, coriander and flour and cook, stirring constantly, for 1 minute more.

3 Cut the courgette slices in half and add to the pan with the corn, chickpeas, tomato purée and vegetable stock. Stir well. Cook for 10 minutes, stirring frequently.

4 Season the stew to taste with salt and pepper. Spoon on to warmed plates and serve immediately with mashed potato.

Cook's Tip
To make garlic mash, add 4–6 finely chopped or crushed garlic cloves to the potatoes about 15 minutes after they began boiling. Reserve 30–45ml/2–3 tbsp of the cooking liquid when you drain the potatoes. Heat a little milk with the reserved liquid, add a little butter and remove the pan from the heat. Add the potatoes and garlic and mash well with a potato masher. Beat with a wooden spoon and season with salt and pepper.

Stew Energy 288kcal/1211kJ; Protein 11.2g; Carbohydrate 42g, of which sugars 12.3g; Fat 9.5g, of which saturates 1.3g; Cholesterol 0mg; Calcium 88mg; Fibre 7.3g; Sodium 388mg.
Stir-fry Energy 2442kcal/10069kJ; Protein 10.2g; Carbohydrate 46.4g, of which sugars 11.8g; Fat 247.4g, of which saturates 55.9g; Cholesterol 53mg; Calcium 96mg; Fibre 7g; Sodium 190mg.

Vegetables with Lentil Bolognese

Instead of the more traditional cheese sauce, it makes a pleasant change to top lightly steamed vegetables with a delicious lentil sauce.

Serves 6

1 small cauliflower broken
 into florets
225g/8oz/2 cups broccoli florets
2 leeks, thickly sliced
225g/8oz Brussels sprouts, halved
 if large

**For the lentil Bolognese
sauce**
45ml/3 tbsp olive oil

1 onion, chopped
2 garlic cloves, crushed
2 carrots, coarsely grated
2 celery sticks, chopped
115g/4oz/1/2 cup red lentils
400g/14oz can
 chopped tomatoes
30ml/2 tbsp tomato
 purée (paste)
450ml/3/4 pint/2 cups vegetable
 stock
15ml/1 tbsp fresh marjoram,
 chopped, or 5ml/1 tsp
 dried marjoram
salt and ground black pepper

1 First make the lentil Bolognese sauce. Heat the oil in a large pan over low heat. Add the onion, garlic, carrots and celery and cook, stirring occasionally, for about 5 minutes, until softened but not coloured.

2 Increase the heat to medium and add the lentils, tomatoes, tomato purée, stock and marjoram. Bring the mixture to the boil, then lower the heat, partially cover the pan with a lid and simmer gently for 20–30 minutes, until the sauce is thick and soft. Season to taste with salt and pepper

3 Meanwhile, place the cauliflower, broccoli, leeks and Brussels sprouts in a steamer set over a pan of boiling water, cover and cook for 8–10 minutes, until all the vegetables are just tender but still have a little crunch.

4 Drain the vegetables and place in a warmed, shallow serving dish. Spoon the lentil Bolognese sauce on top, stir lightly to mix and serve immediately.

Black Bean & Vegetable Stir-fry

This colourful and very flavoursome vegetable mixture is coated in a classic Chinese sauce.

Serves 4
8 spring onions (scallions)
225g/8oz button
 (white) mushrooms
1 red (bell) pepper

1 green (bell) pepper
2 large carrots
60ml/4 tbsp sesame oil
2 garlic cloves, crushed
60ml/4 tbsp black bean sauce
90ml/6 tbsp warm water
225g/8oz/scant 3 cups
 beansprouts
salt and ground black pepper

1 Thinly slice the spring onions and button mushrooms. Set aside in separate bowls.

2 Cut both the peppers in half, remove and discard the seeds and slice the flesh into thin strips.

3 Cut the carrots in half. Cut each half into thin strips lengthways. Stack the slices and cut through them to make very fine strips.

4 Heat the oil in a large wok or frying pan until very hot. Add the spring onions and garlic and stir-fry for 30 seconds.

5 Add the mushrooms, peppers and carrots. Stir-fry over high heat for a further 5–6 minutes, until just beginning to soften.

6 Mix the black bean sauce with the water. Add to the wok or frying pan and cook for a further 3–4 minutes. Stir in the beansprouts and stir-fry for a final 1 minute, until all the vegetables are coated in the sauce. Season to taste with salt and pepper. Serve immediately.

> **Cook's Tip**
> Black bean sauce is available in jars and cans. Once opened it should be stored in the refrigerator.

Bolognese Energy 195kcal/817kJ; Protein 11.8g; Carbohydrate 20.5g, of which sugars 8.8g; Fat 7.8g, of which saturates 1.3g; Cholesterol 0mg; Calcium 83mg; Fibre 7.2g; Sodium 46mg.
Stir-fry Energy 196kcal/817kJ; Protein 6.5g; Carbohydrate 16.1g, of which sugars 9.4g; Fat 12.2g, of which saturates 1.9g; Cholesterol 0mg; Calcium 45mg; Fibre 4.6g; Sodium 19mg.

Tomato & Okra Stew

Okra is an unusual and delicious vegetable. It releases a sticky sap when cooked, which helps to thicken the stew.

Serves 4

15ml/1 tbsp olive oil

1 onion, chopped
400g/14oz can pimientos, drained
2 x 400g/14oz cans
    chopped tomatoes
275g/10oz okra
30ml/2 tbsp chopped
    fresh parsley
salt and ground black pepper

1 Heat the oil in a pan over medium heat. Add the onion and cook, stirring occasionally, for 2–3 minutes, until it is just beginning to soften.

2 Coarsely chop the pimientos and add to the onion. Add the tomatoes with their can juices and mix well.

3 Cut the tops off the okra and cut into halves or quarters if large. Add them to the pan. Season to taste with plenty of salt and pepper.

4 Bring the vegetable stew to the boil, then lower the heat, cover the pan with a tight-fitting lid and simmer gently for about 12 minutes, until all the vegetables are tender and the sauce has thickened. Stir in the chopped parsley, transfer to a warmed serving dish and serve immediately.

Cook's Tip
Okra, also known as bhindi, gumbo and ladies' fingers, is now available all year round. Do not buy pods any longer than 7.5–10cm/3–4in as larger ones tend to be fibrous. Look for clean, dark green pods – a brown tinge indicates staleness. They should feel firm and slightly springy when squeezed and should snap easily, not bend. Store them in the salad drawer of the refrigerator where they will keep for a few days. When preparing, if the ridges look tough or damaged, scrape them with a sharp knife.

Chunky Vegetable Paella

This Spanish rice dish is now enjoyed the world over. This version includes aubergine and chickpeas.

Serves 6

large pinch of saffron threads
1 aubergine (eggplant), cut into
    thick chunks
90ml/6 tbsp olive oil
1 large onion, thickly sliced
3 garlic cloves, crushed
1 yellow (bell) pepper, seeded
    and sliced

1 red (bell) pepper, seeded
    and sliced
10ml/2 tsp paprika
225g/8oz/1¼ cups Valencia or
    risotto rice
600ml/1 pint/2½ cups vegetable
    stock
450g/1lb fresh tomatoes, peeled
    and chopped
115g/4oz mushrooms, sliced
115g/4oz/scant ½ cup cut
    green beans
400g/14oz can chickpeas

1 Place the saffron in a small bowl, add 45ml/3 tbsp hot water and set aside to steep.

2 Place the aubergine chunks in a colander, sprinkle with salt and leave to drain for 30 minutes. Rinse thoroughly under cold running water and pat dry with kitchen paper.

3 Heat the oil in a large paella or frying pan over low heat. Add the onion, garlic, yellow and red peppers and aubergine and cook, stirring occasionally, for about 5 minutes, until the onion has softened but not coloured. Sprinkle in the paprika and stir well.

4 Increase the heat to medium and mix in the rice, then pour in the vegetable stock and add the tomatoes. Stir in the saffron with its soaking water. Season well with salt and pepper. Bring the mixture to the boil, then lower the heat and simmer gently for about 15 minutes, uncovered, shaking the pan frequently and stirring occasionally.

5 Stir in the mushrooms, green beans and chickpeas with their can juices. Simmer gently for a further 10 minutes, then serve hot, direct from the pan.

Stew Energy 122kcal/515kJ; Protein 4.8g; Carbohydrate 16.7g, of which sugars 15.6g; Fat 4.6g, of which saturates 0.9g; Cholesterol 0mg; Calcium 152mg; Fibre 7g; Sodium 97mg.
Paella Energy 385kcal/1610kJ; Protein 11g; Carbohydrate 54.5g, of which sugars 12g; Fat 14.2g, of which saturates 2g; Cholesterol 0mg; Calcium 79mg; Fibre 7.7g; Sodium 160mg.

Onion & Gruyère Tart

The secret of this tart is to cook the onions very slowly until they almost caramelize.

Serves 4
175g/6oz/1½ cups plain (all-purpose) flour
pinch of salt
75g/3oz/6 tbsp butter, diced
1 egg yolk

For the filling
50g/2oz/4 tbsp butter

450g/1lb onions, thinly sliced
15–30ml/1–2 tbsp wholegrain mustard
2 eggs, plus 1 egg yolk
300ml/½ pint/1 cup double (heavy) cream
75g/3oz/¾ cup grated Gruyère cheese
pinch of freshly grated nutmeg
salt and ground black pepper

1 To make the pastry, sift the flour and salt into a bowl. Add the butter and rub it into the flour with your fingertips until the mixture resembles fine breadcrumbs. Add the egg yolk and 15ml/1 tbsp cold water and mix to a firm dough. Chill in the refrigerator for 30 minutes.

2 Preheat the oven to 200°C/400°F/Gas 6. Knead the dough, then roll it out on a lightly floured work surface and use to line a 23cm/9in loose-based flan tin (pan). Prick the base all over with a fork, line the pastry case (pie shell) with baking parchment and fill with baking beans.

3 Bake the pastry case blind for 15 minutes. Remove the paper and beans and bake for a further 10–15 minutes, until the pastry case is crisp. Meanwhile, melt the butter in a pan, add the onions, cover with a tight-fitting lid and cook over low heat, stirring occasionally, for 20 minutes, until golden.

4 Reduce the oven temperature to 180°C/350°F/Gas 4. Spread the pastry case with mustard and top with the onions. Mix together the eggs, egg yolk, cream, cheese and nutmeg and season with salt and pepper. Pour over the onions. Bake for 30–35 minutes, until golden. Remove the tart from the oven and leave to cool slightly. Serve warm.

Potato & Spinach Gratin

Pine nuts add a satisfying crunch to this gratin of wafer-thin potato slices and spinach in a wonderfully creamy cheese sauce.

Serves 2
450g/1lb potatoes
1 garlic clove, crushed
3 spring onions (scallions), thinly sliced

150ml/¼ pint/⅔ cup single (light) cream
250ml/8fl oz/1 cup milk
225g/8oz frozen chopped spinach, thawed
115g/4oz/1 cup grated mature (sharp) Cheddar cheese
25g/1oz/¼ cup pine nuts
salt and ground black pepper
lettuce and tomato salad, to serve

1 Peel the potatoes and cut them carefully into wafer-thin slices. This is most easily done with a mandoline or the slicing attachment of a food processor. Spread the slices out in a large, heavy, non-stick frying pan.

2 Sprinkle the crushed garlic and sliced spring onions evenly over the potatoes.

3 Mix together the cream and milk in a jug (pitcher) and pour the mixture over the potatoes. Place the pan over low heat, cover with a tight-fitting lid and cook for 8 minutes, or until the potatoes are tender.

4 Drain the spinach thoroughly, then, using both hands, squeeze it as dry as possible. Add the spinach to the potatoes, mixing lightly. Cover the pan with a tight-fitting lid and cook for 2 minutes more.

5 Season to taste with salt and pepper, then spoon the mixture into a gratin dish. Preheat the grill (broiler).

6 Sprinkle the grated cheese and pine nuts evenly over the potato and spinach mixture. Lightly toast under the grill for 2–3 minutes, until the cheese has melted and the topping is golden brown. Serve the gratin immediately with a lettuce and tomato salad.

Tart Energy 904kcal/3746kJ; Protein 15g; Carbohydrate 36.7g, of which sugars 3g; Fat 78.2g, of which saturates 47g; Cholesterol 384mg; Calcium 272mg; Fibre 1.6g; Sodium 383mg.
Gratin Energy 527kcal/2212kJ; Protein 28.1g; Carbohydrate 45.3g, of which sugars 11.7g; Fat 27.3g, of which saturates 11.6g; Cholesterol 79mg; Calcium 413mg; Fibre 5.1g; Sodium 183mg.

Linguine with Pesto Sauce

Pesto, the famous Italian basil sauce, originates in Liguria, where the sea breezes are said to give the local basil a particularly fine flavour. Pesto is traditionally made with a pestle and mortar, but it is easier to make in a food processor or blender.

Serves 5–6
65g/2¹/₂ oz fresh basil leaves
3–4 garlic cloves, peeled
45ml/3 tbsp pine nuts
75ml/5 tbsp extra virgin
 olive oil
50g/2oz/scant ³/₄ cup freshly
 grated Parmesan cheese
60ml/4 tbsp freshly grated
 Pecorino cheese
salt and ground black pepper
500g/1¹/₄ lb linguine pasta

1 Place the basil leaves, garlic cloves, pine nuts, 2.5ml/½ tsp salt and olive oil in a food processor or blender and process until smooth. Transfer to a bowl.

2 Stir in the Parmesan and Pecorino cheeses and stir to combine thoroughly. Season to taste with salt and pepper.

3 Bring a large pan of lightly salted water the boil and cook the linguine until it is al dente. Just before draining the pasta, take out about 60ml/4 tbsp of the cooking water and stir it into the pesto sauce.

4 Drain the pasta and toss with the sauce. Serve at once, with extra cheese if wished.

Cook's Tip
• *Pecorino cheese is not as widely available as Parmesan. If you cannot find it, use all Parmesan instead. For the best flavour, buy a piece of Parmesan and grate it yourself.*
• *Pesto sauce is handy to have as a standby in the freezer. It's a good idea to freeze the pesto in an ice cube tray so that you can use as little or as much as you like. Freeze at the end of step 1, before adding the cheese.*

Broccoli & Ricotta Cannelloni

A vegetarian version of an Italian favourite, this pasta dish is the perfect dish for an informal gathering.

Serves 4
12 dried cannelloni tubes,
 7.5cm/3in long
450g/1lb/4 cups broccoli florets
75g/3oz/1¹/₂ cups fresh
 breadcrumbs
150ml/¹/₄ pint/²/₃ cup milk
60ml/4 tbsp olive oil, plus extra
 for brushing
225g/8oz/1 cup ricotta cheese
pinch of freshly grated nutmeg

90ml/6 tbsp freshly grated
 Parmesan or Pecorino cheese
salt and ground black pepper
30ml/2 tbsp pine nuts,
 for sprinkling

For the tomato sauce
1 onion, finely chopped
1 garlic clove, crushed
30ml/2 tbsp olive oil
2 x 400g/14oz cans chopped
 tomatoes
15ml/1 tbsp tomato purée
 (paste)
4 black olives, pitted and chopped
5ml/1 tsp dried thyme

1 Preheat the oven to 190°C/375°F/Gas 5 and grease an ovenproof dish. Bring a pan of water to the boil, add a little olive oil and simmer the pasta, uncovered, until nearly cooked.

2 Meanwhile, boil the broccoli until tender. Drain the pasta and rinse under cold water. Drain the broccoli, then process in a food processor or blender until smooth.

3 Mix together the breadcrumbs, milk and oil in a bowl. Add the ricotta, broccoli purée, nutmeg and 60ml/4 tbsp Parmesan cheese. Season to taste with salt and pepper.

4 To make the sauce, fry the onions and garlic in the oil for 5 minutes. Stir in the tomatoes, tomato purée, olives, thyme and seasoning. Simmer for 2 minutes, then pour into the dish.

5 Open the pasta tubes and, holding them upright on the work surface, pipe in the filling using a 1cm/½in piping nozzle. Arrange in the dish on top of the sauce. Brush with olive oil, then sprinkle over the remaining cheese and the pine nuts. Bake for 30 minutes, or until golden on top. Serve immediately.

Linguine Energy 476kcal/2000kJ; Protein 17.6g; Carbohydrate 56.1g, of which sugars 2.9g; Fat 21.7g, of which saturates 5.6g; Cholesterol 18mg; Calcium 258mg; Fibre 2.6g; Sodium 217mg.
Cannelloni Energy 808kcal/3387kJ; Protein 33.6g; Carbohydrate 80.8g, of which sugars 12.9g; Fat 41.2g, of which saturates 13.4g; Cholesterol 48mg; Calcium 436mg; Fibre 7.1g; Sodium 501mg.

Pasta with Spring Vegetables

Pasta tossed with broccoli, leeks, asparagus and fennel makes an attractive dish, bursting with fresh flavours.

Serves 4
115g/4oz/1 cup broccoli florets
115g/4oz baby leeks
225g/8oz asparagus
1 small fennel bulb
115g/4oz/1 cup fresh or frozen
  peas
40g/1½ oz/3 tbsp butter
1 shallot, chopped
45ml/3 tbsp mixed chopped fresh
  herbs, such as parsley, thyme
  and sage
300ml/½ pint/1¼ cups double
  (heavy) cream
350g/12oz/3 cups dried penne
  pasta
salt and ground black pepper
freshly grated Parmesan cheese,
  to serve

1 Divide the broccoli florets into tiny sprigs. Cut the leeks and asparagus diagonally into 5cm/2in lengths. Trim the fennel bulb and remove any tough outer leaves. Cut into wedges, leaving the layers attached at the root ends so the pieces stay intact.

2 Cook each vegetable separately in boiling salted water until just tender – use the same water for each vegetable. Drain well and keep warm.

3 Melt the butter in a separate pan, add the chopped shallot and cook, stirring occasionally, until softened but not browned. Stir in the herbs and cream and cook for a few minutes, until slightly thickened.

4 Meanwhile, bring a large pan of lightly salted water to the boil and cook the penne for 10 minutes or until *al dente*. Drain well and add to the cream sauce with all the vegetables. Toss gently to combine and season to taste with plenty of pepper. Serve immediately, with plenty of grated Parmesan cheese.

> **Cook's Tip**
> *If you are not keen on the aniseed taste of fennel, you can use a small onion instead. Prepare in the same way.*

Spinach & Hazelnut Lasagne

Hazelnuts add a delicious crunchy texture to the spinach layer of this wholesome lasagne.

Serves 4
900g/2lb/8 cups fresh spinach
300ml/½ pint/1¼ cups vegetable
  stock
1 onion, finely chopped
1 garlic clove, crushed
75g/3oz/¾ cup hazelnuts
30ml/2 tbsp chopped fresh basil
6 sheets no pre-cook lasagne
400g/14oz can chopped
  tomatoes
250ml/8fl oz/1 cup mascarpone
  or fromage frais
salt and ground black pepper
flaked hazelnuts and chopped
  fresh parsley

1 Preheat the oven to 200°C/400°F/Gas 6. Wash the spinach and place in a pan with just the water that clings to the leaves. Cook over high heat for 2 minutes until wilted. Drain well.

2 Heat 30ml/2 tbsp of the stock in a pan and simmer the onion and garlic until soft. Stir in the spinach, hazelnuts and chopped fresh basil.

3 Arrange a layer of the spinach mixture in a large rectangular ovenproof dish. Top with a layer of lasagne, then a layer of chopped tomatoes, seasoning with salt and pepper as you work. Continue in this way, finishing with a layer of pasta.

4 Pour in the remaining stock, then spread the mascarpone or fromage frais over the top. Bake for 45 minutes. Serve hot, sprinkled with hazelnuts and chopped parsley.

> **Cook's Tip**
> *If you're short of time, use frozen spinach instead of fresh – you will need 450g/1lb.*

Vegetables Energy 767kcal/3196kJ; Protein 16.5g; Carbohydrate 64g, of which sugars 7.8g; Fat 51.3g, of which saturates 30.6g; Cholesterol 124mg; Calcium 138mg; Fibre 7.8g; Sodium 93mg.
Lasagne Energy 442kcal/1853kJ; Protein 19.6g; Carbohydrate 48.8g, of which sugars 12.3g; Fat 19.9g, of which saturates 4.8g; Cholesterol 5mg; Calcium 501mg; Fibre 8.6g; Sodium 350mg.

Pasta with Roasted Pepper Sauce

A touch of chilli powder gives this delicious pepper and tomato sauce a slight kick. Serve with a rocket salad for a tasty supper.

Serves 4
2 red (bell) peppers
2 yellow (bell) peppers
45ml/3 tbsp olive oil

1 onion, sliced
2 garlic cloves, crushed
2.5ml/1/2 tsp mild chilli powder
400g/14oz can chopped plum
  tomatoes
450g/1lb/4 cups dried pasta
  shells or spirals
salt and ground black pepper
freshly grated Parmesan cheese,
  to serve

1 Preheat the oven to 200°C/400°F/Gas 6. Place the peppers on a baking sheet and bake for about 20 minutes, or until they are beginning to char and blister. Alternatively, grill (broil) the peppers, turning them from time to time.

2 Rub the skins off the peppers under cold water, or place the charred peppers in a bowl, cover with kitchen paper and leave to cool for 10 minutes, then peel off the skins. Halve the skinned peppers, remove the seeds and roughly chop the flesh.

3 Heat the oil in a pan and cook the onion and garlic gently for 5 minutes, until soft and golden.

4 Stir in the chilli powder, cook for 2 minutes, then add the tomatoes and peppers. Bring to the boil and simmer for about 10–15 minutes, until slightly thickened and reduced. Season with salt and pepper to taste.

5 Bring a large pan of lightly salted water to the boil and cook the pasta until al dente. Drain well and toss with the sauce. Serve piping hot with lots of freshly grated Parmesan cheese.

> **Variation**
> Add other vegetables such as French beans or courgettes (zucchini) or even chickpeas to make the dish more substantial.

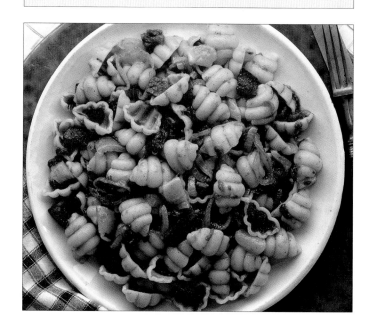

Spaghetti with Herb Sauce

Fresh herbs make a wonderful aromatic sauce – the heat from the pasta releases their flavour to delicious effect. Serve with chunks of warm ciabatta.

Serves 4
50g/2oz chopped mixed fresh
  herbs such as parsley, basil
  and thyme

2 garlic cloves, crushed
60ml/4 tbsp pine nuts, toasted
150ml/1/4 pint/2/3 cup olive oil
350g/12oz dried spaghetti
60ml/4 tbsp freshly grated
  Parmesan cheese
salt and ground black pepper
fresh basil leaves, to garnish

1 Put the herbs, garlic and half the pine nuts into a food processor or blender. With the machine running slowly, add the oil and process to form a thick purée.

2 Bring a large pan of lightly salted water to the boil and cook the spaghetti until al dente. Drain thoroughly.

3 Transfer the herb purée to a large warm bowl, then add the spaghetti and Parmesan. Toss well to coat the pasta with the sauce. Season with salt and pepper.

4 Sprinkle the remaining pine nuts and the basil leaves over the pasta and serve immediately.

> **Cook's Tip**
> When cooking long strands of pasta like spaghetti, drop one end of the pasta into the boiling water and, as it softens, push it down gently until it bends in the middle and is completely immersed. Refer to the packet instructions for cooking times as these can vary from type to type. As a general rule, dried pasta needs 8–10 minutes. Do not be tempted to overcook pasta; it should be cooked until al dente, that is, until is it is tender but still firm to the bite. Always test the pasta just before you think it should be ready, to avoid overcooking.

Spaghetti Energy 699kcal/2924kJ; Protein 18.9g; Carbohydrate 65.8g, of which sugars 3.8g; Fat 41.9g, of which saturates 7.5g; Cholesterol 15mg; Calcium 229mg; Fibre 3.5g; Sodium 171mg.
Pasta Energy 537kcal/2273kJ; Protein 16.1g; Carbohydrate 98.9g, of which sugars 18.3g; Fat 11.3g, of which saturates 1.7g; Cholesterol 0mg; Calcium 53mg; Fibre 7.3g; Sodium 20mg.

Pasta Rapido with Parsley Pesto

This fresh, lively sauce will stir the appetite and pep up any pasta supper. Made with parsley and almonds, it makes a tasty change from the more familiar basil and pine nut pesto.

Serves 4–6
450g/1lb/4 cups dried pasta
75g/3oz/¾ cup whole almonds
50g/2oz/½ cup flaked (sliced)
  almonds toasted
25g/1oz/⅓ cup freshly grated
  Parmesan cheese
pinch of salt

For the sauce
40g/1½oz fresh flat leaf parsley
2 garlic cloves, crushed
45ml/3 tbsp olive oil
45ml/3 tbsp lemon juice
5ml/1 tsp sugar
250ml/8fl oz/1 cup boiling water

1 Bring a large pan of lightly salted water to the boil and cook the pasta until *al dente*.

2 Meanwhile, toast the whole and flaked almonds separately under a medium grill (broiler) until golden brown. Set the flaked almonds aside.

3 To make the sauce, chop the parsley finely in a food processor. Add the whole almonds and reduce to a fine consistency. Add the garlic, olive oil, lemon juice, sugar and water. Process to make a sauce.

4 Drain the pasta and transfer to a warmed serving bowl. Add half of the sauce and toss to combine well. (Keep the rest of the sauce for another dish.) Top with freshly grated Parmesan cheese and the reserved flaked almonds, and serve.

> **Cook's Tip**
> The unused parsley pesto sauce will keep in a screw-top jar in the refrigerator for up to ten days. Serve it with any type of cooked pasta or try using the sauce as a topping for lightly cooked broccoli or grilled polenta.

Macaroni Cheese with Mushrooms

An old favourite is given a new twist with the addition of mushrooms and a light sprinkling of pine nuts. It is finished off under the grill to give a glorious golden top.

Serves 4
450g/1lb/4 cups quick-cooking
  dried elbow macaroni
45ml/3 tbsp olive oil
225g/8oz button (white)
  mushrooms, sliced
2 fresh thyme sprigs
50g/2oz/4 tbsp plain
  (all-purpose) flour
1 vegetable stock cube
600ml/1 pint/2½ cups milk
2.5ml/½ tsp celery salt
5ml/1 tsp Dijon mustard
175g/6oz/1½ cups grated
  Cheddar cheese
25g/1oz/⅓ cup freshly grated
  Parmesan cheese
25g/1oz/¼ cup pine nuts
salt and ground black pepper

1 Bring a large pan of lightly salted water to the boil and cook the macaroni until *al dente*.

2 Meanwhile, heat the oil in a heavy pan, add the mushrooms and thyme, cover and cook over gentle heat for 2–3 minutes. Stir in the flour and remove from the heat. Add the stock cube and stir continuously until evenly blended. Stir in the milk a little at a time, stirring after each addition.

3 Add the celery salt, mustard and Cheddar cheese and season to taste with salt and pepper. Stir to combine well, then simmer for about 1–2 minutes, stirring continuously, until the sauce has thickened.

4 Preheat the grill (broiler) to medium. Drain the macaroni well, toss into the sauce and turn into four individual dishes or one large flameproof gratin dish. Scatter with grated Parmesan cheese and pine nuts, then grill (broil) until brown and bubbly.

> **Variation**
> Add some finely shredded sun-dried tomatoes and a handful of fresh spinach to the sauce just before adding the macaroni.

Pasta Energy 688kcal/2894kJ; Protein 23.1g; Carbohydrate 87.3g, of which sugars 6.4g; Fat 29.9g, of which saturates 4.1g; Cholesterol 6mg; Calcium 199mg; Fibre 6.2g; Sodium 79mg.
Macaroni Energy 831kcal/3497kJ; Protein 35.2g; Carbohydrate 100.7g, of which sugars 11.4g; Fat 33.9g, of which saturates 14.2g; Cholesterol 58mg; Calcium 628mg; Fibre 4.4g; Sodium 456mg.

Pasta with Tomatoes & Rocket

This pretty-coloured pasta dish relies for its success on the slightly peppery taste of the rocket. It is deliciously fresh tasting. Serve it with chunks of rustic bread and a glass of dry white wine for a perfect lunch dish.

Serves 4
450g/1lb/4 cups dried conchiglie
450g/1lb ripe cherry tomatoes
75g/3oz fresh rocket
45ml/3 tbsp olive oil
salt and ground black pepper
Parmesan cheese shavings,
  to serve

1 Bring a large pan of lightly salted water to the boil and cook the pasta until *al dente*.

2 Meanwhile, halve the tomatoes. Wash and dry the rocket.

3 Heat the oil in a large pan and gently cook the tomatoes for barely 1 minute. The tomatoes should only just be heated through and not be allowed to disintegrate.

4 Drain the pasta and add to the pan, then add the rocket. (Roughly tear any rocket leaves that are over-large.) Carefully stir to mix and heat through. Season to taste with salt and pepper. Serve hot, with plenty of shaved Parmesan cheese.

Cook's Tip
Rocket has a distinctive peppery taste that is useful for adding character to all sorts of salad dishes. It is increasingly available in supermarkets. However, if you have difficulty finding it, why not grow your own: it is very easy to grow in the garden or even in a window-box, and this will ensure that you have a plentiful supply to hand.

Variation
Add a crushed garlic clove to the pan with the tomatoes, or just add a dash of balsamic vinegar for added flavour.

Fettuccine all'Alfredo

A classic from Rome, this dish is simply pasta tossed with cream, butter and freshly grated Parmesan cheese. It makes a great supper dish, served with a crisp green salad to cut through the richness.

Serves 4
25g/1oz/2 tbsp butter
150ml/¼ pint/⅔ cup double (heavy) cream, plus
  60ml/4 tbsp extra
450g/1lb dried fettuccine
50g/2oz/scant ¾ cup freshly grated Parmesan cheese, plus
  extra to serve
pinch of freshly grated nutmeg
salt and ground black pepper

1 Place the butter and 150ml/¼ pint/⅔ cup cream in a heavy pan. Bring to the boil, then simmer for 1 minute until the mixture has slightly thickened.

2 Bring a large pan of lightly salted water to the boil and cook the fettuccine until it is *al dente* – it should still be a little firm to the bite.

3 Drain the pasta very thoroughly and return to the pan with the cream sauce.

4 Place the pan on the heat and turn the pasta in the sauce to coat it evenly.

5 Add the remaining cream, the Parmesan cheese, salt and pepper to taste and a little grated nutmeg. Toss until well coated and heated through. Serve immediately with some extra grated Parmesan cheese sprinkled on top.

Variations
For a little extra colour, fresh or frozen peas make an attractive addition to the sauce. You could also try stirring in thin strips of ham if you are not catering for vegetarians. The fettuccine ribbons can be replaced by spaghetti very successfully.

Tomatoes & Rocket Energy 483kcal/2044kJ; Protein 14.8g; Carbohydrate 87.2g, of which sugars 7.5g; Fat 10.8g, of which saturates 1.5g; Cholesterol 0mg; Calcium 68mg; Fibre 4.8g; Sodium 40mg.
Fettuccine Energy 674kcal/2830kJ; Protein 19.1g; Carbohydrate 84g, of which sugars 4.4g; Fat 31.4g, of which saturates 18.6g; Cholesterol 77mg; Calcium 198mg; Fibre 3.3g; Sodium 186mg.

Feta & Roasted Garlic Pizzettes

These pizzettes are for garlic lovers. Mash down the cloves as you eat them – they should be meltingly soft and sweet-tasting.

Serves 4

1 garlic bulb, unpeeled
45ml/3 tbsp olive oil
1 red (bell) pepper, seeded
  and quartered
1 yellow (bell) pepper, seeded
  and quartered
2 plum tomatoes
1 quantity Basic Pizza Dough (see
  below left)
175g/6oz/1½ cups crumbled
  feta cheese
pinch of black pepper
15–30ml/1–2 tbsp chopped fresh
  oregano, to garnish

1 Preheat the oven to 220°C/425°F/Gas 7. Break the garlic into cloves, discarding the outer papery layers. Toss in 15ml/1 tbsp of the olive oil.

2 Place the peppers skin-side up on a baking sheet and grill (broil), turning them until the skins are evenly charred. Place in a covered bowl for 10 minutes, then peel off the skins. Cut the flesh into strips.

3 Make a slash in the skin of each tomato, then put them in a bowl and pour over boiling water. Leave for 30 seconds, then plunge into cold water. Peel, seed and roughly chop the flesh.

4 Divide the pizza dough into four pieces and roll out each one on a lightly floured surface to an equal-sized circle of about 13cm/5in diameter. Place the dough circles well apart on two greased baking sheets, then push up the dough edges to form a thin rim around the dough circles.

5 Brush the dough circles with half the remaining oil and scatter over the chopped tomatoes. Top with the peppers, crumbled feta cheese and garlic cloves. Drizzle over the remaining oil and season to taste with pepper.

6 Bake in the oven for 15–20 minutes until crisp and golden. Garnish with chopped oregano and serve immediately.

Onion & Gorgonzola Pizzas

These small pizzas are good for snacks or party food.

Serves 4

1 quantity Basic Pizza Dough
  (see below)
30ml/2 tbsp garlic oil
2 small red onions
150g/5oz Gorgonzola cheese,
  rind removed and diced
2 garlic cloves, cut into strips
  lengthways
10ml/2 tsp chopped fresh sage
pinch of black pepper

1 Preheat the oven to 220°C/425°F/Gas 7. Divide the dough into eight pieces and roll out to small ovals about 5mm/¼in thick. Place well apart on two greased baking sheets and prick with a fork. Brush well with 15ml/1 tbsp of the garlic oil.

2 Halve, then slice the onions into thin wedges. Scatter over the pizza bases. Sprinkle with the cheese, then the garlic and sage. Drizzle the remaining oil on top and grind over plenty of pepper. Bake for 10–15 minutes until crisp and golden.

Basic Pizza Dough

Making your own pizza base is easy – and it tastes great.

Makes one 25–30cm/10–12in round pizza base

175g/6oz/1½ cups strong white
  flour
1.25ml/¼ tsp salt
5ml/1 tsp easy-blend (rapid-rise)
  dried yeast
120–150ml/4–5fl oz/½–¾ cup
  lukewarm water
15ml/1 tbsp olive oil

1 Sift the flour and salt into a large mixing bowl and stir in the yeast. Make a well in the centre and pour in the water and oil. Mix to a soft dough. Knead the dough on a lightly floured board for 10 minutes until smooth and elastic.

2 Place in a greased bowl, cover with clear film (plastic wrap) and leave to double in size for about 1 hour. Turn out on to a floured surface; knead gently for 2–3 minutes. Use as required.

Pizzas Energy 371kcal/1550kJ; Protein 12.5g; Carbohydrate 38g, of which sugars 3.5g; Fat 19.8g, of which saturates 8.5g; Cholesterol 28mg; Calcium 263mg; Fibre 2.2g; Sodium 461mg.
Pizza Dough Energy 696kcal/2944kJ; Protein 16.4g; Carbohydrate 136g, of which sugars 2.6g; Fat 13.3g, of which saturates 1.9g; Cholesterol 0mg; Calcium 245mg; Fibre 5.4g; Sodium 5mg.
Pizzettes Energy 419kcal/1751kJ; Protein 14.1g; Carbohydrate 45.9g, of which sugars 8.6g; Fat 21.1g, of which saturates 7.8g; Cholesterol 31mg; Calcium 234mg; Fibre 4.3g; Sodium 640mg.

Wild Mushroom Pizzas

With their delicate earthy flavour, wild mushrooms make a delicious topping for these little pizzas. Serve as an unusual starter or for a stylish light meal.

Serves 4

45ml/3 tbsp olive oil
350g/12oz fresh mixed wild
    mushrooms, washed and sliced

2 shallots, chopped
2 garlic cloves, finely chopped
30ml/2 tbsp chopped fresh mixed
    thyme and flat leaf parsley
1 quantity Basic Pizza Dough
    (see page 65)
40g/1½ oz/generous ¼ cup
    grated Gruyère cheese
30ml/2 tbsp freshly grated
    Parmesan cheese
salt and ground black pepper

1 Preheat the oven to 220°C/425°F/Gas 7. Heat 30ml/2 tbsp of the oil in a frying pan and fry the mushrooms, shallots and garlic over medium heat, stirring occasionally, until all the juices have evaporated.

2 Stir in half the herbs and season with salt and pepper then set aside to cool.

3 Divide the dough into four pieces and roll out each one on a lightly floured surface to a 13cm/5in circle. Place well apart on two greased baking sheets, then push up the dough edges to form a thin rim around the dough circles.

4 Brush the pizza bases with the remaining oil and spoon the wild mushrooms on top. Mix together the Gruyère and Parmesan, then sprinkle over the mushroom mixture.

5 Bake the pizza for 15–20 minutes until crisp and golden. Remove from the oven and scatter over the remaining herbs.

Cook's Tip
Fresh wild mushrooms add a distinctive flavour to the topping, but if they are unavailable, a mixture of cultivated mushrooms, such as shiitake, oyster and chestnut, would do just as well.

Rocket & Tomato Pizza

Peppery rocket leaves and aromatic basil add colour and flavour to this pizza.

Serves 2

10ml/2 tsp olive oil, plus extra
    for oiling and drizzling
1 garlic clove, crushed
150g/5oz/1 cup canned chopped
    tomatoes
2.5ml/½ tsp sugar
30ml/2 tbsp torn basil leaves
2 tomatoes, seeded and chopped

150g/5oz/⅔ cup mozzarella
    cheese, sliced
20g/¾oz/1 cup rocket leaves
rock salt and ground black pepper

For the pizza base

225g/8oz/2 cups strong white
    bread flour, sifted
5ml/1 tsp salt
2.5ml/½ tsp easy-blend
    (rapid-rise) dried yeast
15ml/1 tbsp olive oil
150ml/¼ pint/⅔ cup warm water

1 To make the pizza base, place the flour, salt and yeast in a bowl. Make a well in the centre and add the oil and warm water. Mix to form a soft dough.

2 Turn out the dough on to a lightly floured work surface and knead for 5 minutes. Cover with the upturned bowl and leave to rest for about 5 minutes, then knead for a further 5 minutes until the dough is smooth and elastic. Place in a lightly oiled bowl and cover with clear film (plastic wrap). Leave in a warm place for about 45 minutes until doubled in size.

3 Preheat the oven to 220°C/425°F/Gas 7. To make the topping, heat the oil in a frying pan and fry the garlic for 1 minute. Add the tomatoes and sugar and cook for 5–7 minutes until reduced and thickened. Stir in the basil and season to taste with salt and pepper. Set aside.

4 Knead the risen dough lightly, then roll out to form a rough 30cm/12in round. Place on a lightly oiled baking sheet and push up the edges of the dough to form a shallow, even rim. Spoon the tomato mixture over the pizza base, then top with the fresh tomatoes and mozzarella. Adjust the seasoning and drizzle with a little olive oil. Bake for 10–12 minutes until crisp and golden. Arrange the rocket over the pizza just before serving.

Rocket Energy 735Kcal/3087kJ; Protein 26.1g; Carbohydrate 93g, of which sugars 7.3g; Fat 31.3g, of which saturates 12.7g; Cholesterol 44mg; Calcium 459mg; Fibre 5.5g; Sodium 330mg.
Mushroom Energy 340kcal/1425kJ; Protein 11.4g; Carbohydrate 35.6g, of which sugars 1.7g; Fat 17.8g, of which saturates 5.5g; Cholesterol 17mg; Calcium 234mg; Fibre 2.5g; Sodium 160mg.

Fiorentina Pizza

Fresh spinach is the star ingredient of this pizza. A grating of nutmeg heightens its flavour.

Serves 2–3
1 quantity Basic Pizza Dough
  (see page 65)
175g/6oz/1½ cups fresh spinach
45ml/3 tbsp olive oil
1 small red onion, thinly sliced
1 jar ready-made tomato sauce or
  pizza topping
pinch of freshly grated nutmeg
150g/5oz mozzarella cheese
1 egg
25g/1oz/¼ cup grated Gruyère
  cheese

1 Preheat the oven to 220°C/425°F/Gas 7. Roll out the pizza dough to a 25–30cm/10–12in circle and place on a greased baking sheet. Push up the edge of the dough to form a thin rim.

2 Remove the stalks from the spinach and wash the leaves in plenty of cold water. Drain well and pat dry with kitchen paper.

3 Heat 15ml/1 tbsp of the oil in a large frying pan and fry the onion until softened. Add the spinach and continue to fry until just wilted. Drain off any excess liquid.

4 Brush the pizza base with half the remaining oil. Spread over the tomato sauce or pizza topping, then top with the spinach mixture. Grate over some nutmeg.

5 Thinly slice the mozzarella cheese and arrange over the spinach. Drizzle over the remaining oil. Bake for 10 minutes, then remove from the oven.

6 Make a small well in the centre of the pizza and drop the egg into the hole. Sprinkle over the Gruyère and return to the oven for a further 5–10 minutes until crisp and golden.

> **Cook's Tip**
> The egg adds the finishing touch to this spinach pizza. Try not to overcook it, as it is best when the yolk is still slightly soft.

Classic Margherita Pizza

Bought pizza base mixes are a great storecupboard stand-by, but you can use the basic pizza dough recipe on page 65 if you prefer. A Margherita Pizza makes a lovely simple supper, but of course you can add any extra toppings you like. Fresh herbs are a simple, but very tasty option.

Serves 2
half a 300g/11oz packet pizza
  base mix, or ready-made base
15ml/1 tbsp herb-infused olive oil
45ml/3 tbsp ready-made tomato
  and basil sauce
150g/5oz mozzarella, sliced
salt and ground black pepper
fresh basil leaves, to garnish

1 Make the pizza base mix (if using) according to the instructions on the packet. Brush the base with a little of the herb-infused olive oil and spread over the tomato and basil sauce, not quite to the edges.

2 Arrange the slices of mozzarella on top of the pizza and bake for 25–30 minutes, or until golden.

3 Drizzle the remaining oil on top of the pizza, season with salt and black pepper and serve immediately, garnished with fresh basil leaves.

> **Variations**
> There are endless possibilities for vegetarian pizza toppings to add to a Margherita. Here are a few to get you started:
> • Roasted vegetables, such as aubergine (eggplant), red and yellow (bell) peppers, courgette (zucchini) and red onion are delicious on top of a Margherita pizza and even better with some goat's cheese crumbled on top.
> • Black olives give a simple twist to a classic pizza.
> • Ricotta and fontina cheeses combined with mushrooms and oregano make a delicious creamy topping for pizza.
> • Chunks of butternut squash roasted with finely chopped shallot and fresh sage leaves make a more unusual topping.

Fiorentina Energy 515kcal/2150kJ; Protein 20.9g; Carbohydrate 40.8g, of which sugars 5.2g; Fat 30.8g, of which saturates 11.4g; Cholesterol 104mg; Calcium 415mg; Fibre 3.2g; Sodium 634mg.
Margherita Energy 420kcal/1761kJ; Protein 7.6g; Carbohydrate 49.8g, of which sugars 7.8g; Fat 22.6g, of which saturates 2.2g; Cholesterol 2mg; Calcium 133mg; Fibre 3.4g; Sodium 130mg.

Marinara Pizza

The combination of garlic, good quality olive oil and oregano gives this pizza an unmistakably Italian flavour.

Serves 2–3
1 quantity Basic Pizza Dough
  (see page 65)

675g/1½ lb ripe plum tomatoes
60ml/4 tbsp extra virgin olive oil
4 garlic cloves, cut into slivers
15ml/1 tbsp chopped fresh
  oregano
salt and ground black pepper

1 Roll out the pizza dough to a 25–30cm/10–12in circle and place on a greased baking sheet. Push up the edge of the dough to form a thin rim around the dough circle.

2 Make a slash in the skin of each tomato, then put them all in a heatproof bowl and pour over boiling water. Leave for 30 seconds, then plunge the tomatoes into cold water. Peel and seed, then roughly chop the flesh.

3 Preheat the oven to 220°C/425°F/Gas 7. Heat 30ml/2 tbsp of the oil in a pan. Add the tomatoes and cook, stirring frequently, for about 5 minutes until soft.

4 Place the tomatoes in a metal sieve (strainer) and leave them to drain for about 5 minutes. Transfer the tomatoes to a food processor or blender and purée until smooth.

5 Brush the pizza base with half the remaining oil. Spoon over the tomatoes and sprinkle with garlic and oregano. Drizzle over the remaining oil and season to taste.

6 Bake for 15–20 minutes until crisp. Serve immediately.

> **Cook's Tip**
> Ready-made pizza bases are handy if you are short of time. They are available from most supermarkets and come in a range of sizes. It is useful to keep a few in the freezer.

Quattro Formaggi

Rich and cheesy, these individual pizzas are quick to make, and the aroma of melting cheese is irresistible.

Serves 4
1 quantity Basic Pizza Dough
  (see page 65)
15ml/1 tbsp garlic oil
½ small red onion, very thinly
  sliced

50g/2oz Dolcelatte cheese
50g/2oz mozzarella cheese
50g/2oz/½ cup grated Gruyère
  cheese
30ml/2 tbsp freshly grated
  Parmesan cheese
15ml/1 tbsp chopped fresh thyme
ground black pepper

1 Preheat the oven to 220°C/425°F/Gas 7. Divide the dough into four pieces and roll out each one on a lightly floured surface into a 13cm/5in circle. Place well apart on two greased baking sheets, then push up the dough edges to make a thin rim. Brush with garlic oil and top with the red onion.

2 Cut the Dolcelatte and mozzarella cheeses into dice and arrange over the bases. Mix together the Gruyère, Parmesan and thyme and sprinkle over the pizzas.

3 Grind plenty of pepper over the pizzas. Bake for 15–20 minutes until the base is crisp and golden and the cheeses are bubbling. Serve immediately.

> **Cook's Tip**
> To make garlic oil, put 3–4 peeled garlic cloves in a jar and pour in 120ml/4fl oz/½ cup olive oil. Cover tightly and store in the refrigerator for up to 1 month.

> **Variation**
> Any variety of cheese that melts readily can be used, but a mixture of soft and hard cheeses gives the best result.

Marinara Energy 415kcal/1742kJ; Protein 8.1g; Carbohydrate 54.5g, of which sugars 8.1g; Fat 19.8g, of which saturates 3g; Cholesterol 0mg; Calcium 100mg; Fibre 4.6g; Sodium 23mg.
Formaggi Energy 397kcal/1661kJ; Protein 14.6g; Carbohydrate 39.7g, of which sugars 3.9g; Fat 20.8g, of which saturates 9.3g; Cholesterol 37mg; Calcium 283mg; Fibre 2.3g; Sodium 405mg.

Aubergine & Shallot Calzone

Aubergines, shallots and sun-dried tomatoes make an unusual filling for calzone.

Serves 2

4 baby aubergines (eggplants)
45ml/3 tbsp olive oil
3 shallots, chopped
1 garlic clove, chopped
6 pieces sun-dried tomatoes in oil, drained and chopped
1.5ml/¼ tsp dried red chilli flakes
10ml/2 tsp chopped fresh thyme
1 quantity Basic Pizza Dough (see page 65)
75g/3oz/generous ½ cup diced mozzarella cheese
salt and ground black pepper
15–30ml/1–2 tbsp freshly grated Parmesan cheese, to serve

1 Preheat the oven to 220°C/425°F/Gas 7. Trim the baby aubergines, then cut into small dice.

2 Heat 30ml/2 tbsp oil in a heavy frying pan. Add the shallots and fry over low heat, stirring occasionally, for 5 minutes until softened by not browned.

3 Add the aubergines, garlic, sun-dried tomatoes, red chilli flakes and thyme to the shallots and season with salt and pepper. Cook for 4–5 minutes, stirring frequently, until the aubergine is beginning to soften.

4 Divide the dough in half and roll out each piece on a lightly floured surface to an 18cm/7in circle. Spread the aubergine mixture over half of each circle, leaving a 2.5cm/1in border, then arrange the mozzarella on top.

5 Dampen the edges with water, then fold the dough over to enclose the filling. Press the edges firmly together to seal. Place on two greased baking sheets.

6 Brush with half the remaining oil and make a small hole in the top of each to allow the steam to escape. Bake for about 15–20 minutes until golden. Remove from the oven and brush with the remaining oil. Sprinkle over the Parmesan and serve the calzone immediately.

Okra Fried Rice

This spicy rich dish gains its creamy consistency from the natural juices of the sliced okra.

Serves 3–4

30ml/2 tbsp vegetable oil
15g/½ oz/1 tbsp butter or margarine
1 garlic clove, crushed
½ red onion, finely chopped
115g/4oz okra, topped and tailed
30ml/2 tbsp diced green and red (bell) peppers
2.5ml/½ tsp dried thyme
2 green chillies, finely chopped
2.5ml/½ tsp five-spice powder
1 vegetable stock cube
30ml/2 tbsp soy sauce
15ml/1 tbsp chopped fresh coriander (cilantro)
225g/8oz/2½ cups cooked rice
salt and ground black pepper
fresh coriander sprigs, to garnish

1 Heat the oil and butter or margarine in a frying pan or wok and cook the garlic and onion over medium heat for 5 minutes until softened.

2 Thinly slice the okra, add to the pan or wok and sauté gently for 6–7 minutes.

3 Add the green and red peppers, thyme, chillies and five-spice powder. Cook gently for 3 minutes, then crumble in the vegetable stock cube.

4 Add the soy sauce, coriander and rice and heat through, stirring well. Season to taste with salt and pepper. Serve hot, garnished with coriander sprigs.

Cook's Tips
• Okra is a five-sided green pod with a tapering end. When buying okra, choose small firm pods that are brightly coloured. Avoid any that are bendy and browning at the edges or tips.
• When preparing chillies, wear rubber gloves if possible, as chillies contain a substance that burns sensitive skin. Wash the knife, board and your hands (if not protected) after preparation. Never rub your eyes or touch your lips after handling chillies.

Aubergine Energy 672kcal/2814kJ; Protein 20.5g; Carbohydrate 75.6g, of which sugars 7.8g; Fat 34.1g, of which saturates 10.3g; Cholesterol 29mg; Calcium 378mg; Fibre 7.4g; Sodium 240mg.
Fried Rice Energy 175kcal/731kJ; Protein 2.8g; Carbohydrate 20.6g, of which sugars 2.6g; Fat 9.6g, of which saturates 0.9g; Cholesterol 0mg; Calcium 62mg; Fibre 1.5g; Sodium 568mg.

Root Vegetable Couscous

Harissa is a very fiery Tunisian chilli sauce which is now available ready-made from larger supermarkets.

Serves 4
350g/12oz/2¼ cups couscous
45ml/3 tbsp olive oil
4 baby onions, halved
675g/1½lb fresh mixed root vegetables such as carrots, swede (ratabega), turnip, celeriac and sweet potatoes, cubed
2 garlic cloves, crushed
pinch of saffron threads
2.5ml/½ tsp each ground cinnamon and ginger
2.5ml/½ tsp ground turmeric
5ml/1 tsp each ground cumin and coriander
15ml/1 tbsp tomato purée (paste)
450ml/¾ pint/scant 2 cups hot vegetable stock
1 small fennel bulb, quartered
115g/4oz/1 cup cooked or canned chickpeas
50g/2oz/½ cup seedless raisins
30ml/2 tbsp chopped fresh coriander (cilantro)
30ml/2 tbsp chopped fresh flat leaf parsley
salt and ground black pepper

For the spiced sauce
15ml/1 tbsp olive oil
15ml/1 tbsp lemon juice
15ml/1 tbsp chopped fresh coriander (cilantro)
2.5–5ml/½–1 tsp harissa

1 Put the couscous in a bowl, cover with hot water, then drain. Heat the oil in a frying pan and gently fry the onions for 3 minutes. Add the root vegetables and fry for 5 minutes. Add the garlic and spices and cook for 1 minute, stirring.

2 Transfer the vegetable mixture to a large deep pan. Stir in the tomato purée, stock, fennel, chickpeas, raisins, chopped coriander and flat leaf parsley. Bring to the boil. Put the couscous into a muslin-lined steamer and place this over the vegetable mixture. Cover and simmer for 20 minutes, or until the vegetables are tender.

3 To make the sauce, put 250ml/8fl oz/1 cup of the vegetable liquid in a bowl and mix with all of the sauce ingredients.

4 Spoon the couscous on to a plate and pile the vegetables on top. Serve at once, handing round the sauce separately.

Risotto with Mushrooms

The addition of wild mushrooms gives a lovely woody flavour to this dish.

Serves 4
25g/1oz dried wild mushrooms, preferably porcini
350ml/12fl oz/1½ cups warm water
900ml/1½ pints/3¾ cups vegetable stock
175g/6oz fresh cultivated mushrooms
juice of ½ lemon
75g/3oz/6 tbsp butter
30ml/2 tbsp finely chopped fresh parsley
30ml/2 tbsp olive oil
1 small onion, finely chopped
275g/10oz/1½ cups arborio risotto rice
120ml/4fl oz/½ cup dry white wine
45ml/3 tbsp freshly grated Parmesan cheese
salt and ground black pepper

1 Place the dried mushrooms in a small bowl with the warm water. Leave to soak for at least 40 minutes. Remove the mushrooms and rinse, then filter the soaking water through a sieve (strainer) lined with kitchen paper into a pan. Add the stock and leave to simmer until needed.

2 Slice the fresh mushrooms. Toss with the lemon juice. Melt a third of the butter in a large frying pan. Stir in the mushrooms and cook until they begin to brown. Stir in the parsley, cook for 30 seconds more, then transfer to a side dish.

3 Heat another third of the butter with the olive oil in the mushroom pan and cook the onion until golden. Add the rice and stir for 1–2 minutes. Add all the mushrooms. Pour in the wine and cook until it has evaporated.

4 Add a ladleful of the hot stock and stir gently until it has been absorbed. Continue adding a ladleful of stock at a time, until all the stock has been absorbed and the rice is tender and creamy.

5 Remove the risotto pan from the heat. Stir in the remaining butter and the Parmesan. Grind in a little pepper, and taste again for salt; adjust if necessary. Allow the risotto to rest for 3–4 minutes before serving.

Couscous Energy 444kcal/1855kJ; Protein 9.5g; Carbohydrate 75.1g, of which sugars 24.2g; Fat 13.5g, of which saturates 1.8g; Cholesterol 0mg; Calcium 115mg; Fibre 7.5g; Sodium 131mg.
Risotto Energy 518kcal/2150kJ; Protein 10.6g; Carbohydrate 56.5g, of which sugars 1.2g; Fat 25.2g, of which saturates 12.9g; Cholesterol 51mg; Calcium 161mg; Fibre 0.7g; Sodium 240mg.

Tomato Risotto

This pretty risotto makes a lovely summery meal, served with a chilled white wine.

Serves 4

675g/1½ lb firm ripe tomatoes
50g/2oz/¼ cup butter
1 onion, finely chopped
1.2 litres/2 pints/5 cups vegetable stock
275g/10oz/1½ cups arborio rice
400g/14oz can cannellini beans, drained
50g/2oz/½ cup finely grated Parmesan cheese
salt and ground black pepper
10–12 fresh basil leaves, shredded and freshly grated Parmesan cheese, to serve

1 Halve the tomatoes and scoop out the seeds into a sieve (strainer) placed over a bowl. Press the seeds with a spoon to extract all the juice. Set the juuice aside.

2 Grill (broil) the tomatoes skin-side up until evenly charred and blistered. Rub off the skins and dice the flesh.

3 Melt the butter in a large frying pan and cook the onion for 5 minutes until beginning to soften. Add the tomatoes and the reserved juice. Season with salt and pepper, then cook, stirring occasionally, for about 10 minutes. Meanwhile, bring the vegetable stock to the boil in another pan.

4 Add the rice to the tomatoes and stir to coat, then add a ladleful of the stock and stir gently until it has been absorbed. Continue adding a ladleful of stock at a time, until all the stock has been absorbed and the rice is tender and creamy.

5 Stir in the cannellini beans and grated Parmesan and heat through for a few minutes. Just before serving the risotto, sprinkle each portion with shredded basil leaves and Parmesan.

> **Cook's Tip**
> If possible, use plum tomatoes in this dish, as they have a fresh, vibrant flavour and meaty texture.

Grilled Polenta with Peppers

Golden slices of herby polenta taste delicious topped with yellow and red pepper strips, heightened with balsamic vinegar.

Serves 4

2 red (bell) peppers
2 yellow (bell) peppers
115g/4oz/scant 1 cup polenta
25g/1oz/2 tbsp butter
15–30ml/1–2 tbsp mixed chopped herbs such as parsley, thyme and sage
melted butter, for brushing
60ml/4 tbsp olive oil
1–2 garlic cloves, cut into slivers
15ml/1 tbsp balsamic vinegar
salt and ground black pepper
fresh herb sprigs, to garnish

1 Preheat the oven to 200°C/400°F/Gas 6. Place the peppers on a baking sheet and bake for about 20 minutes or until they are beginning to char and blister.

2 Put the charred peppers in a bowl, cover and leave to cool for 10 minutes, then peel off the skins. Remove the seeds and cores, then cut the flesh into strips. Set aside.

3 Bring 600ml/1 pint/2½ cups salted water to the boil in a heavy pan. Trickle in the polenta, beating continuously, then cook gently for 15–20 minutes, stirring occasionally, until the mixture is no longer grainy and comes away from the sides of the pan.

4 Remove the pan from the heat and beat in the butter, chopped herbs and plenty of pepper. Pour the polenta into a pudding bowl, smooth the surface and leave until cold and firm.

5 Turn out the polenta on to a board and cut into thick slices. Brush the polenta slices with melted butter and grill (broil) each side for about 4–5 minutes, until golden brown.

6 Meanwhile, heat the olive oil in a frying pan, add the garlic and peppers and stir-fry for 1–2 minutes. Stir in the balsamic vinegar and season with salt and pepper.

7 Spoon the pepper mixture over the polenta slices and garnish with fresh herb sprigs. Serve immediately.

Risotto Energy 531kcal/2220kJ; Protein 18.4g; Carbohydrate 79.2g, of which sugars 9.8g; Fat 15.9g, of which saturates 9.4g; Cholesterol 39mg; Calcium 252mg; Fibre 8.1g; Sodium 618mg.
Polenta Energy 309kcal/1280kJ; Protein 4.6g; Carbohydrate 32.5g, of which sugars 10.7g; Fat 17.8g, of which saturates 5g; Cholesterol 13mg; Calcium 16mg; Fibre 3.5g; Sodium 45mg.

Asparagus & Cheese Risotto

It's important to use arborio rice for this Italian dish in order to achieve the creamy texture that is characteristic of an authentic risotto.

Serves 4

1.5ml/¼ tsp saffron threads
750ml/1¼ pints/3 cups hot
   vegetable stock
25g/1oz/2 tbsp butter
30ml/2 tbsp olive oil
1 large onion, finely chopped
2 garlic cloves, finely chopped
225g/8oz/1¼ cups arborio
   risotto rice
300ml/½ pint/1¼ cups dry white
   wine
225g/8oz asparagus tips, cooked
75g/3oz/1 cup freshly grated
   Parmesan cheese
salt and ground black pepper
fresh Parmesan cheese shavings,
   to garnish
ciabatta bread rolls and green
   salad, to serve

1 Sprinkle the saffron over the stock and leave to infuse for 5 minutes. Heat the butter and oil in a frying pan and fry the onion and garlic for about 6 minutes until softened.

2 Add the rice and stir-fry for 1–2 minutes to coat the grains with the butter and oil. Pour on 300ml/½ pint/1¼ cups of the stock and saffron. Cook gently, stirring frequently, until the liquid is absorbed. Repeat with another 300ml/½ pint/1¼ cups stock. When that is absorbed, add the wine and continue to cook, stirring, until the rice has a creamy consistency.

3 Add the asparagus and remaining stock, and stir until the liquid is absorbed and the rice is tender. Stir in the Parmesan cheese and season to taste with salt and pepper.

4 Spoon the risotto on to warmed plates and garnish with the Parmesan cheese shavings. Serve immediately with hot ciabatta rolls and a mixed green salad.

> **Cook's Tip**
> *If preferred, you can use whole asparagus spears, cut into 5cm/2in lengths, but the stems should not be too thick.*

Lemon & Herb Risotto Cake

This unusual rice dish can be served as a light main course with salad, or as a satisfying side dish.

Serves 4

1 small leek, thinly sliced
600ml/1 pint/2½ cups
   vegetable stock
225g/8oz/1¼ cups risotto rice
finely grated rind of 1 lemon
30ml/2 tbsp chopped fresh chives
30ml/2 tbsp chopped
   fresh parsley
75g/3oz/generous ½ cup grated
   mozzarella cheese
salt and ground black pepper
fresh parsley and lemon wedges,
   to garnish

1 Preheat the oven to 200°C/400°F/Gas 6. Lightly oil a 22cm/8½in round loose-bottomed cake tin (pan).

2 Put the sliced leek in a large pan with 45ml/3 tbsp of the stock. Cook over medium heat, stirring occasionally, for about 5 minutes until softened. Add the rice and the remaining stock.

3 Bring to the boil. Lower the heat, cover the pan with a tight-fitting lid and simmer gently, stirring occasionally, for about 20 minutes, or until all the liquid has been absorbed.

4 Stir in the lemon rind, chives, chopped parsley and grated mozzarella cheese and season with salt and pepper to taste. Spoon into the tin, cover with foil and bake for 30–35 minutes or until lightly browned.

5 Carefully turn out the risotto cake and cut into slices. Serve immediately, garnished with parsley and lemon wedges.

> **Cook's Tips**
> • *This risotto cake is equally delicious served cold, so it makes ideal picnic food. Chill until needed, then pack layered with kitchen foil or baking parchment.*
> • *If you cannot obtain risotto rice, use short grain rice – the type normally used for puddings – instead.*

Asparagus Risotto Energy 473kcal/1969kJ; Protein 14.2g; Carbohydrate 52.4g, of which sugars 5.8g; Fat 17.5g, of which saturates 8g; Cholesterol 32mg; Calcium 278mg; Fibre 2g; Sodium 248mg.
Lemon Risotto Energy 260kcal/1086kJ; Protein 8.4g; Carbohydrate 46g, of which sugars 0.9g; Fat 4.4g, of which saturates 2.6g; Cholesterol 11mg; Calcium 110mg; Fibre 1.2g; Sodium 79mg.

Bulgur & Lentil Pilaff

Many of the ingredients for this tasty, aromatic dish can be found in a well-stocked store cupboard.

Serves 4
5ml/1 tsp olive oil
1 large onion, thinly sliced
2 garlic cloves, crushed
5ml/1 tsp ground coriander
5ml/1 tsp ground cumin
5ml/1 tsp ground turmeric
2.5ml/½ tsp ground allspice
225g/8oz/1¼ cups bulgur wheat
about 750ml/1¼ pints/3 cups
    vegetable stock or water
115g/4oz/1½ cups sliced button
    (white) mushrooms
115g/4oz/½ cup green lentils
cayenne pepper
salt and ground black pepper
fresh parsley sprigs, to garnish

1 Heat the oil in a non-stick pan and fry the onion, garlic, ground coriander, cumin, turmeric and allspice and fry over low heat, stirring constantly, for 1 minute.

2 Stir in the bulgur wheat and cook, stirring constantly, for about 2 minutes, until lightly browned. Add the stock or water, mushrooms and lentils.

3 Bring to the boil, cover, then simmer over very low heat for 25–30 minutes, until the bulgur wheat and lentils are tender and all the liquid has been absorbed. Add more stock or water during cooking, if necessary.

4 Season well with salt, black pepper and cayenne pepper. Transfer to a warmed serving dish and serve immediately, garnished with parsley sprigs.

Cook's Tips
• *Bulgur wheat is very easy to cook and can be used in almost any way you would normally use rice – hot or cold. Some of the finer grades need hardly any cooking, so check the packet instructions for cooking times.*
• *Green lentils can be cooked without presoaking. They cook quite quickly and keep their shape.*

Minted Couscous Castles

These pretty little timbales are perfect for serving as part of a summer lunch. They are virtually fat-free, so you can happily indulge yourself without feeling remotely guilty.

Serves 6
225g/8oz/1¼ cups couscous
475ml/16fl oz/2 cups boiling
    vegetable stock
15ml/1 tbsp lemon juice
2 tomatoes, diced
30ml/2 tbsp chopped fresh mint
oil, for brushing
salt and ground black pepper
fresh mint sprigs, to garnish

1 Place the couscous in a bowl and pour over the boiling stock. Cover the bowl and leave to stand for 30 minutes, until all the stock has been absorbed and the grains are tender.

2 Stir in the lemon juice with the tomatoes and chopped mint. Adjust the seasoning with salt and pepper.

3 Brush the insides of four cups or individual moulds lightly with oil. Spoon in the couscous mixture and pack down firmly. Chill for several hours.

4 Invert the castles on to a platter and serve cold, garnished with mint. Alternatively, cover and heat gently in a low oven, then turn out and serve hot.

Cook's Tip
You will need the "instant" type of couscous for this dish, which is now widely available from most supermarkets. However, this type of quick couscous is not always immediately distinguishable from traditional couscous, which requires steaming first, so always check the instructions on the packet before buying. Only Moroccan couscous is produced in this "instant" form. The grains of traditional couscous can vary in size depending on the country of origin; the grains of Moroccan couscous are small, whereas Lebanese couscous is about the size of chickpeas.

Pilaff Energy 242kcal/1016kJ; Protein 11.3g; Carbohydrate 47g, of which sugars 3.2g; Fat 2.1g, of which saturates 0.2g; Cholesterol 0mg; Calcium 45mg; Fibre 3.6g; Sodium 7mg.
Castles Energy 94kcal/396kJ; Protein 2.7g; Carbohydrate 20.7g, of which sugars 1g; Fat 0.5g, of which saturates 0g; Cholesterol 0mg; Calcium 27mg; Fibre 0.3g; Sodium 4mg.

Red Fried Rice

In this delicious version of egg fried rice, the vibrant colours of red onion, red pepper and cherry tomatoes add lots of eye appeal. An ideal dish for a quick supper.

Serves 2

115g/4oz/¾ cup basmati rice

30ml/2 tbsp groundnut (peanut) oil
1 small red onion, chopped
1 red (bell) pepper, seeded and chopped
225g/8oz cherry tomatoes, halved
2 eggs, beaten
salt and ground black pepper

1 Rinse the rice several times under cold running water. Drain well. Bring a large pan of water to the boil, add the rice and cook for 10–12 minutes.

2 Meanwhile, heat the oil in a wok until very hot and stir-fry the onion and red pepper for 2–3 minutes. Add the cherry tomatoes and stir-fry for a further 2 minutes.

3 Pour in the beaten eggs all at once. Cook for 30 seconds without stirring, then stir to break up the eggs as they set.

4 Drain the cooked rice thoroughly, add to the wok and toss it over the heat with the vegetable and egg mixture for 3 minutes. Season the fried rice with salt and pepper to taste.

Cook's Tips
• Basmati rice is good for this dish as its slightly crunchy texture complements the softness of the egg.
• It is possible to stir-fry in a frying pan, if you don't have a wok. However, the heat will be less evenly distributed and it is harder to toss the ingredients.

Variation
Add diced cheese or tofu with dashes of soy sauce.

Fruity Brown Rice

An oriental-style dressing gives this colourful rice salad extra piquancy.

Serves 4

115g/4oz/⅔ cup brown rice
1 small red (bell) pepper, seeded and diced
200g/7oz can sweetcorn kernels, drained
45ml/3 tbsp sultanas (golden raisins)

225g/8oz can pineapple pieces in fruit juice
15ml/1 tbsp light soy sauce
15ml/1 tbsp sunflower oil
15ml/1 tbsp hazelnut oil
1 garlic clove, crushed
5ml/1 tsp finely chopped fresh root ginger
salt and ground black pepper
4 spring onions (scallions), diagonally sliced, to garnish

1 Bring a large pan of lightly salted water to the boil and cook the brown rice for about 30 minutes, or until it is just tender. Drain thoroughly, rinse under cold water and drain again. Set aside to cool.

2 Turn the rice into a large serving bowl and add the red pepper, sweetcorn and sultanas. Drain the pineapple pieces, reserving the juice, then add to the rice mixture and toss lightly.

3 Pour the reserved pineapple juice into a clean screw-top jar. Add the soy sauce, sunflower and hazelnut oils, garlic and chopped root ginger. Season to taste with salt and pepper. Close the jar tightly and shake vigorously to combine.

4 Pour the dressing over the salad and toss well. Scatter the spring onions over the top and serve.

Cook's Tip
• Hazelnut oil gives a distinctive flavour to any salad dressing. Like olive oil, it contains mainly mono-unsaturated fats.
• Brown rice is often mistakenly called wholegrain. In fact, the outer husk is completely inedible and is removed from all rice, but the bran layer is left intact on brown rice.

Red Rice Energy 437kcal/1821kJ; Protein 12.6g; Carbohydrate 57.4g, of which sugars 10.5g; Fat 17.6g, of which saturates 3.1g; Cholesterol 190mg; Calcium 62mg; Fibre 3g; Sodium 85mg.
Fruity Rice Energy 189kcal/797kJ; Protein 3g; Carbohydrate 35.5g, of which sugars 14.4g; Fat 4.8g, of which saturates 0.6g; Cholesterol 0mg; Calcium 18mg; Fibre 1.9g; Sodium 272mg.

Nut Pilaff with Omelette Rolls

This pilaff fuses together a wonderful mixture of textures – soft fluffy rice with crunchy nuts and omelette rolls.

Serves 2
175g/6oz/1 cup basmati rice
15ml/1 tbsp sunflower oil
1 small onion, chopped

1 red (bell) pepper, finely diced
350ml/12fl oz/1½ cups hot
    vegetable stock
2 eggs
25g/1oz/¼ cup salted peanuts
15ml/1 tbsp soy sauce
salt and ground black pepper
fresh parsley sprigs, to garnish

1 Rinse the rice several times under cold running water. Drain thoroughly and set aside.

2 Heat half the oil in a large frying pan and fry the onion and red pepper for 2–3 minutes, then stir in the rice and stock. Bring to the boil, lower the heat slightly and simmer for 10 minutes until the rice is tender.

3 Meanwhile, beat the eggs lightly and season to taste with salt and pepper. Heat the remaining oil in a second large frying pan. Pour in the eggs and tilt the pan to cover the base thinly. Cook the omelette for 1 minute, then flip it over and cook the other side for 1 minute.

4 Slide the omelette on to a clean board and roll it up tightly. Cut the omelette roll into eight slices.

5 Stir the peanuts and the soy sauce into the pilaff and add black pepper to taste. Turn the pilaff into a serving dish, then carefully arrange the omelette rolls on top and garnish with the parsley. Serve immediately.

> **Variation**
> To ring the changes, try salted cashew nuts or toasted flaked almonds instead of the peanuts.

Aubergine Pilaff

This hearty dish is made with bulgur wheat and aubergine, flavoured with fresh mint. It is a perfect choice for a midweek supper as it can be prepared within 15 minutes.

Serves 2
2 aubergines (eggplants)
60–90ml/4–6 tbsp sunflower oil
1 small onion, finely chopped

175g/6oz/1 cup bulgur wheat
450ml/¾ pint/scant 2 cups
    vegetable stock
30ml/2 tbsp pine nuts, toasted
15ml/1 tbsp chopped fresh mint
salt and ground black pepper

For the garnish
lime wedges
lemon wedges
fresh mint sprigs

1 Trim the ends from the aubergines, then slice them lengthways. Cut each slice into neat sticks and then into 1cm/½in dice.

2 Heat 60ml/4 tbsp of the oil in a large heavy frying pan, add the onion and fry over medium heat for 1 minute. Add the the diced aubergine. Increase the heat to high and cook, stirring frequently, for about 4 minutes until just tender. Add the remaining oil if needed.

4 Stir in the bulgur wheat, mixing well, then pour in the vegetable stock. Bring to the boil, then lower the heat and simmer for 10 minutes or until all the liquid has evaporated. Season to taste with salt and pepper.

5 Stir in the pine nuts and mint, then spoon the pilaff on to individual plates. Garnish each portion with lime and lemon wedges. Sprinkle with torn mint leaves for extra colour and serve immediately.

> **Variation**
> Use courgettes (zucchini) instead of aubergine, or for something completely different, substitute pumpkin or acorn squash.

Nut Energy 550kcal/2292kJ; Protein 17.4g; Carbohydrate 80g, of which sugars 8.4g; Fat 17.7g, of which saturates 3.4g; Cholesterol 190mg; Calcium 69mg; Fibre 2.6g; Sodium 609mg.
Aubergine Energy 542kcal/2248kJ; Protein 9.6g; Carbohydrate 52.2g, of which sugars 5.3g; Fat 34g, of which saturates 3.5g; Cholesterol 0mg; Calcium 83mg; Fibre 3.7g; Sodium 7mg.

Strawberries in Spiced Grape Jelly

Strawberries set in a fruity jelly delicately flavoured with cinnamon makes this the ideal dessert to serve after a filling main course.

Serves 4

450ml/¾ pint/scant 2 cups red
grape juice
1 cinnamon stick
1 small orange
15ml/1 tbsp powdered vegetarian gelatine
225g/8oz/2 cups strawberries, chopped, plus extra to decorate

1 Place the grape juice in a pan with the cinnamon stick. Thinly pare the rind from the orange. Add most of it to the pan, but shred some pieces and set them aside for the decoration.

2 Place the pan over very low heat heat for 10 minutes, then remove the cinnamon stick and orange rind.

3 Squeeze the juice from the orange into a bowl and sprinkle over the powdered gelatine. Stir into the grape juice until the gelatine has completely dissolved. Allow to cool until just starting to set.

4 Stir in the strawberries, then quickly turn the mixture into a 1 litre/1¾ pint/4 cup mould or serving dish. Chill until set.

5 To serve, dip the mould quickly into hot water and turn the jelly out on to a serving plate. Decorate with whole strawberries and the reserved shreds of orange rind.

Cook's Tip

Do not wash the strawberries until just before you hull them. Dip them quickly in water, then pat dry on kitchen paper.

Variation

Use a different flavoured fruit juice, such as cranberry juice.

Plum & Port Sorbet

This sophisticated sorbet is deliciously refreshing.

Serves 4

900g/2lb ripe red plums, stoned (pitted) and halved
75g/3oz/6 tbsp caster (superfine) sugar
45ml/3 tbsp ruby port or red wine
crisp sweet cookies, to serve

1 Place the plums in a pan with the sugar and 45ml/3 tbsp water. Stir over low heat until the sugar has melted. Cover and simmer gently for about 5 minutes until the fruit is soft.

2 Turn into a food processor or blender and purée until smooth, then stir in the port or red wine. Cool completely, then turn into a plastic freezer container and freeze until the sorbet is firm around the edges. Process until smooth. Spoon back into the freezer container and freeze until solid.

3 Allow to soften slightly at room temperature for about 15–20 minutes before serving in scoops, with sweet cookies.

Quick Apricot Blender Whip

This is one of the quickest desserts you could make and also one of the prettiest. Decorate with lightly toasted slivered almonds if you like.

Serves 4

400g/14oz can apricot halves
15ml/1 tbsp Grand Marnier or brandy
175ml/6fl oz/¾ cup Greek (US plain strained) yogurt

1 Drain the juice from the apricot halves and place the fruit in a blender or food processor with the Grand Marnier or brandy. Process until smooth.

2 Spoon the fruit purée and the yogurt in alternate spoonfuls into four tall glasses, swirling them together slightly to give a marbled effect. Serve immediately.

Grape Jelly Energy 80kcal/338kJ; Protein 4g; Carbohydrate 16.6g, of which sugars 16.6g; Fat 0.2g, of which saturates 0g; Cholesterol 0mg; Calcium 31mg; Fibre 0.6g; Sodium 11mg.
Sorbet Energy 173kcal/738kJ; Protein 1.5g; Carbohydrate 40.8g, of which sugars 40.8g; Fat 0.2g, of which saturates 0g; Cholesterol 0mg; Calcium 40mg; Fibre 3.6g; Sodium 6mg.
Apricot Whip Energy 117kcal/491kJ; Protein 5.4g; Carbohydrate 11.9g, of which sugars 11.7g; Fat 4.9g, of which saturates 0.6g; Cholesterol 1mg; Calcium 140mg; Fibre 2.3g; Sodium 50mg.

Peach & Ginger Pashka

A low-fat version of the Russian Easter favourite – a glorious cheese dessert flavoured with peaches and preserved stem ginger.

2 pieces preserved stem ginger in syrup, drained and chopped, plus 30ml/2 tbsp syrup from the jar
2.5ml/½ tsp vanilla extract

Serves 4
350g/12oz/1½ cups low-fat cottage cheese
2 peaches or nectarines, peeled
90g/3½oz/scant ½ cup low-fat natural (plain) yogurt

To decorate
1 peach or nectarine, peeled and sliced
10ml/2 tsp slivered almonds, toasted

1 Drain the cottage cheese and rub it through a fine sieve (strainer) into a bowl. Remove the stones (pits) from the peaches or nectarines and roughly chop.

2 Mix together the chopped peaches or nectarines in a large bowl with the low-fat cottage cheese, yogurt, preserved stem ginger and syrup and vanilla extract.

3 Line a new, clean flower pot or a strainer with a piece of clean, fine cloth, such as muslin (cheesecloth).

4 Add the cheese mixture and wrap over the cloth to cover. Place a saucer on top and weigh down. Stand over a bowl in a cool place and leave to drain overnight.

5 To serve, unwrap the cloth and turn the pashka out on to a serving plate. Decorate the pashka with peach or nectarine slices and toasted almonds.

> **Cook's Tip**
> *Rather than making one large pashka, line 4 to 6 cups or ramekins with a clean cloth or muslin and divide the mixture evenly among them.*

Tofu Berry Brulée

If you feel that classic brulée is too rich for you, then this lighter variation is a must. Made from tofu, it is low in fat yet tastes great. Use any soft fruits that are in season.

Serves 4
225g/8oz/2 cups red berry fruits such as strawberries, raspberries and redcurrants
300g/11oz packet silken tofu
45ml/3 tbsp icing (confectioners') sugar
65g/2½ oz/¼ cup demerara (raw) sugar

1 Halve or quarter any large strawberries, but leave the smaller ones whole. Mix with the other chosen berries.

2 Place the tofu and icing sugar in a food processor or blender and process until smooth.

3 Stir in the fruits and spoon into a flameproof dish with a 900ml/1½ pint/3¾ cup capacity. Sprinkle the top with enough demerara sugar to cover evenly.

4 Place under a very hot grill (broiler) until the sugar melts and caramelizes. Chill well before serving.

> **Cook's Tips**
> • *Choose silken tofu rather than firm tofu as it gives a smoother texture in this type of dish. Firm tofu is better for cooking in chunks.*
> • *Tofu is make from soya beans and is a popular vegetarian ingredient as it is a good source of protein. It is bland in taste, but absorbs other flavours well.*

> **Variation**
> *For a more indulgent version, replace the tofu with double (heavy) cream and add a few drops of vanilla extract.*

Brulée Energy 178kcal/754kJ; Protein 6.7g; Carbohydrate 32.7g, of which sugars 32.4g; Fat 3.2g, of which saturates 0.4g; Cholesterol 0mg; Calcium 406mg; Fibre 0.6g; Sodium 8mg.
Pashka Energy 79kcal/334kJ; Protein 9.3g; Carbohydrate 8.6g, of which sugars 8.6g; Fat 1.1g, of which saturates 0.7g; Cholesterol 3mg; Calcium 116mg; Fibre 0.8g; Sodium 197mg.

Berry Frozen Yogurt

A super-easy iced dessert, using frozen summer fruits.

Serves 6
350g/12oz/3 cups frozen
   summer fruits

200ml/7fl oz/scant 1 cup Greek
   (US strained plain) yogurt
25g/1oz/¼ cup icing
   (confectioners') sugar

1 Put all the ingredients into a food processor and process until combined but still quite chunky. Spoon into six 150ml/¼ pint/ ⅔ cup ramekin dishes. Cover with cling film (plastic wrap) and freeze for 2 hours until firm.

2 To turn out, dip briefly in hot water and invert on to individual plates, tapping the bases of the dishes to release the desserts.

Rippled Chocolate Ice Cream

Rich, smooth and packed with chocolate, this heavenly ice cream is a real treat.

Serves 4
60ml/4 tbsp chocolate and
   hazelnut spread

450ml/¾ pint/scant 2 cups
   double (heavy) cream
15ml/1 tbsp icing (confectioners')
   sugar
50g/2oz plain (semisweet)
   chocolate, chopped
chocolate curls, to decorate

1 Mix together the chocolate and hazelnut spread and 75ml/ 5 tbsp of the double cream in a bowl.

2 Place the remaining cream in another bowl, sift in the icing sugar and beat until softly whipped. Lightly fold in the chocolate and hazelnut mixture with the chopped chocolate until the mixture is rippled. Transfer to a plastic freezer container and freeze for 3–4 hours, until firm.

3 Remove from the freezer about 10 minutes before serving. Serve in scoops, topped with a few chocolate curls.

Fruited Rice Ring

This unusual chilled rice pudding ring is topped with a tasty mix of dried fruits that have been simmered until meltingly soft. The delicious combination of the fruits and rice makes this a truly healthy dish.

Serves 4
65g/2½ oz/¼ cup short grain
   pudding rice
900ml/1½ pints/3¾ cups semi-
   skimmed (low-fat) milk
1 cinnamon stick
175g/6oz mixed dried fruit
175ml/6fl oz/¾ cup orange juice
40g/1½oz/3 tbsp caster
   (superfine) sugar
finely grated rind of 1 small
   orange

1 Place the rice, milk and cinnamon stick in a large pan and bring to the boil. Cover and simmer, stirring occasionally, for about 1½ hours, until all the liquid has been absorbed.

2 Meanwhile, place the dried fruit and orange juice in a pan and bring to the boil. Cover and simmer very gently for about 1 hour, until tender and all the liquid has been absorbed.

3 Remove the cinnamon stick from the rice and discard. Stir in the caster sugar and orange rind.

4 Carefully spoon the cooked fruit into the base of a lightly oiled 1.5 litre/2½ pint/6¼ cup ring mould. Spoon the rice over the fruit, smoothing it down firmly. Chill.

5 Run a knife around the edge of the mould and turn out the rice carefully on to a serving plate.

Cook's Tip
Rather than using a ring mould and turning out the dish, you may prefer to serve the dessert straight from individual small dishes. In this case, spoon the cooked rice into 6 dishes, then top with the cooked fruit. Chill well before serving.

Yogurt Energy 71kcal/295kJ; Protein 2.6g; Carbohydrate 8.5g, of which sugars 8.5g; Fat 3.5g, of which saturates 1.7g; Cholesterol 0mg; Calcium 62mg; Fibre 0.7g; Sodium 28mg.
Ice Cream Energy 719kcal/2971kJ; Protein 3.4g; Carbohydrate 22.9g, of which sugars 22.6g; Fat 68.9g, of which saturates 41.2g; Cholesterol 155mg; Calcium 81mg; Fibre 0.4g; Sodium 33mg.
Rice Ring Energy 334kcal/1418kJ; Protein 10.1g; Carbohydrate 67.6g, of which sugars 54.7g; Fat 4.1g, of which saturates 2.4g; Cholesterol 13mg; Calcium 315mg; Fibre 1g; Sodium 123mg.

Apricot Mousse

Dried apricots are used to flavour this delightful, light and airy dessert. Serve in dainty stemmed glass dishes for a pretty effect.

Serves 4

300g/10oz ready-to-eat dried
   apricots

300ml/½ pint/1¼ cups fresh
   orange juice
200g/7oz/¾ cup low-fat Greek
   (US strained plain) yogurt
2 egg whites
fresh mint sprigs, to decorate

1 Place the apricots in a pan with the orange juice and heat gently until boiling. Cover the pan and gently simmer the apricots for 3 minutes.

2 Cool slightly, then place in a food processor or blender and process until smooth. Stir in the Greek yogurt.

3 Whisk the egg whites in a clean, grease-free bowl until stiff enough to hold soft peaks, then fold gently into the puréed apricot mixture.

4 Spoon the mousse into four stemmed glasses or one large serving dish. Chill in the refrigerator before serving, decorated with sprigs of fresh mint.

Cook's Tips
• *This fluffy dessert can be made with any dried fruits instead of apricots – try dried peaches, prunes or apples.*
• *When folding in whisked egg whites, always use a large metal spoon, and employ a light cutting action.*

Variation
To make a speedier, fool-type dessert, omit the egg whites and simply swirl together the apricot mixture and the yogurt.

Apple Foam with Blackberries

A light-as-air dessert, with lots of contrast in colour, flavour and texture, this is the perfect dish for people wanting to cut down on their fat intake.

Serves 4

225g/8oz/2 cups blackberries
150ml/¼ pint/⅔ cup apple juice
5ml/1 tsp powdered vegetarian
   gelatine
15ml/1 tbsp clear honey
2 egg whites

1 Place the blackberries in a pan with 60ml/4 tbsp of the apple juice and heat gently until the fruit is soft. Remove from the heat, cool, then chill in the refrigerator.

2 Sprinkle the gelatine over the remaining apple juice in a small pan and stir over gentle heat until dissolved. Stir in the honey.

3 Whisk the egg whites in a clean, grease-free bowl until stiff peaks form. Continue whisking hard and gradually pour in the hot gelatine mixture until well mixed.

4 Quickly spoon the foam into rough mounds on individual plates. Chill. To serve, spoon the blackberries and juice around the foam rounds.

Cook's Tips
• *Make sure you dissolve the gelatine over very low heat. It must not boil, otherwise it will lose its setting ability.*
• *Use a balloon, rotary or electric whisk to whisk the egg whites. The bowl must be completely clean, any grease will stop the egg whites achieving optimum volume. Do not overbeat the egg whites, this makes them dry and they will not fold evenly.*

Variation
Any seasonal soft fruit can be used to accompany the apple foam if blackberries are not available.

Mousse Energy 180kcal/768kJ; Protein 8.7g; Carbohydrate 37.4g, of which sugars 37.4g; Fat 0.6g, of which saturates 0.1g; Cholesterol 1mg; Calcium 107mg; Fibre 4.8g; Sodium 65mg.
Apple Foam Energy 49kcal/209kJ; Protein 3.1g; Carbohydrate 9.5g, of which sugars 9.5g; Fat 0.2g, of which saturates 0g; Cholesterol 0mg; Calcium 27mg; Fibre 1.8g; Sodium 33mg.

Blackberry Brown Sugar Meringue

A rich dessert which is elegant enough to be served at an autumnal dinner party.

Serves 6
For the meringue
175g/6oz/¾ cup soft light brown
  sugar
3 egg whites
5ml/1 tsp distilled malt vinegar
2.5ml/½ tsp vanilla extract

For the filling
350–450g/12oz–1lb/3–4 cups
  blackberries
30ml/2 tbsp crème de cassis
300ml/½ pint/1¼ cups double
  (heavy) cream
15ml/1 tbsp icing (confectioners')
  sugar, sifted
small blackberry leaves, to
  decorate (optional)

1 Preheat the oven to 160°C/325°F/Gas 3. Draw a 20cm/8in circle on a sheet of non-stick baking parchment, turn over and place on a baking sheet. Spread the brown sugar out on a baking sheet, dry in the oven for 8–10 minutes, then sieve (sift).

2 Whisk the egg whites in a clean, grease-free bowl until stiff. Add half the dried brown sugar, 15g/½oz/1 tbsp at a time, whisking well after each addition. Add the vinegar and vanilla extract, then fold in the remaining sugar.

3 Spoon the meringue on to the drawn circle on the paper, making a hollow in the centre. Bake for 45 minutes, then turn off the oven and leave the meringue in the oven with the door slightly open, until cold. Meanwhile, place the blackberries in a bowl, sprinkle over the crème de cassis and leave to macerate for 30 minutes.

4 When the meringue is cold, carefully peel off the baking parchment and transfer to a serving plate. Lightly whip the cream with the icing sugar and spoon into the centre. Top with the blackberries and decorate with blackberry leaves, if you like.

> **Variation**
> *Fill with a mix of raspberries, strawberries and red currants.*

Clementines in Cinnamon Caramel

The combination of sweet yet sharp clementines and caramel sauce, flavoured with a hint of spice, is divine. Serve with thick yogurt or crème fraîche to make a delicious dessert for family and friends.

Serves 4–6
8–12 clementines
225g/8oz/generous 1 cup sugar
300ml/½ pint/1¼ cups warm
  water
2 cinnamon sticks
30ml/2 tbsp orange-flavoured
  liqueur
25g/1oz/¼ cup shelled
  pistachio nuts

1 Using a vegetable peeler, pare the rind from two clementines, and cut it into fine strips. Set aside.

2 Peel the clementines, removing all the pith but keeping them intact. Put the fruits in a serving bowl.

3 Gently heat the sugar in a pan until it melts and turns a rich golden brown. Immediately turn off the heat.

4 Cover your hand with a dish towel and pour in the warm water (the mixture will bubble violently). Bring slowly to the boil, stirring until the caramel has dissolved. Add the shredded rind and whole cinnamon sticks, then simmer for 5 minutes. Stir in the orange-flavoured liqueur.

5 Leave the syrup to cool for about 10 minutes, then pour over the clementines. Cover the bowl and chill for several hours or overnight.

6 Blanch the pistachios in boiling water. Drain, cool and remove the dark outer skins. Scatter over the clementines and serve.

> **Variation**
> *Use oranges instead of clementines: using a sharp knife, remove the rind and pith, cutting downwards, then slice horizontally.*

Meringue Energy 404kcal/1684kJ; Protein 2.9g; Carbohydrate 36.9g, of which sugars 36.9g; Fat 27g, of which saturates 16.7g; Cholesterol 69mg; Calcium 66mg; Fibre 1.8g; Sodium 45mg.
Clementines Energy 215kcal/912kJ; Protein 1.7g; Carbohydrate 46.8g, of which sugars 46.7g; Fat 2.4g, of which saturates 0.3g; Cholesterol 0mg; Calcium 50mg; Fibre 1.3g; Sodium 28mg.

Chocolate Chestnut Roulade

Don't worry if this moist sponge cracks as you roll it up – this is the sign of a good roulade.

Serves 8

175g/6oz plain (semisweet) chocolate
30ml/2 tbsp strong black coffee
5 eggs, separated
175g/6oz/scant 1 cup caster (superfine) sugar
250ml/8fl oz/1 cup double (heavy) cream
225g/8oz unsweetened chestnut purée
45–60ml/3–4 tbsp icing (confectioners') sugar, plus extra for dusting
single (light) cream, to serve

1 Preheat the oven to 180°C/350°F/Gas 4, then line and oil a 33 x 23cm/13 x 9in Swiss roll tin (jell roll pan); use non-stick baking parchment. Melt the chocolate in a bowl over gently simmering water, then stir in the coffee. Leave to cool slightly.

2 Whisk the egg yolks and caster sugar together until thick and light, then stir in the cooled chocolate mixture. Whisk the egg whites in another clean bowl until stiff. Stir a spoonful into the chocolate mixture to lighten it, then gently fold in the rest.

3 Pour the mixture into the prepared tin and spread level. Bake for 20 minutes. Remove from the oven, cover with a dish towel and leave to cool in the tin for several hours.

4 Whip the double cream until soft peaks begin to form. Mix together the chestnut purée and icing sugar, then fold into the whipped cream.

5 Dust a sheet of greaseproof (waxed) paper with icing sugar. Turn out the roulade on to this paper and peel off the lining paper. Trim the sides. Gently spread the chestnut cream evenly over the roulade to within 2.5cm/1in of the edges. Using the greaseproof paper to help you, carefully roll up the roulade as tightly and evenly as possible.

6 Chill the roulade for about 2 hours, then dust liberally with icing sugar. Serve cut into thick slices with cream poured over.

Pasta Timbales with Apricot Sauce

This unusual dessert is made like a rice pudding, but uses tiny pasta shapes instead of the rice. It looks very attractive.

Serves 4

100g/4oz/1 cup orzo or other small soup pasta
75g/3oz/⅓ cup caster (superfine) sugar
pinch of salt
25g/1oz/2 tbsp butter
1 vanilla pod (bean), split
750ml/1¼ pints/3 cups milk
300ml/½ pint/1¼ cups ready-made custard
45ml/3 tbsp Kirsch
15ml/1 tbsp powdered vegetarian gelatine
oil, for greasing
400g/14oz can apricots in juice
lemon juice to taste
fresh flowers, to decorate (optional)

1 Place the pasta, sugar, pinch of salt, butter, vanilla pod and milk into a heavy pan and bring to the boil. Turn down the heat and simmer for 25 minutes until the pasta is tender and most of the liquid is absorbed. Stir frequently to prevent it from sticking.

2 Remove the vanilla pod and transfer the pasta to a bowl to cool. Stir in the custard and add 30ml/2 tbsp of the kirsch.

3 Sprinkle the gelatine over 45ml/2 tbsp water in a small bowl set in a pan of barely simmering water. Allow to become spongy and heat gently to dissolve. Stir into the pasta.

4 Lightly oil 4 timbale moulds and spoon in the pasta. Chill for 2 hours until set.

5 Meanwhile, purée the apricots in a food processor or blender, then pass through a sieve (strainer) and add lemon juice and Kirsch to taste. Dilute with a little water if too thick.

6 Run a knife around the edge of each timbale to loosen the mixture. To turn out, place an individual plate on the top of each mould, then holding the plate and mould firmly together, invert them. Serve with apricot sauce and decorated with fresh flowers if you wish.

Roulade Energy 469kcal/1961kJ; Protein 6.2g; Carbohydrate 53.5g, of which sugars 44.9g; Fat 27.1g, of which saturates 15.2g; Cholesterol 163mg; Calcium 68mg; Fibre 1.7g; Sodium 57mg.
Timbales Energy 425kcal/1797kJ; Protein 12g; Carbohydrate 67.6g, of which sugars 47.3g; Fat 10.2g, of which saturates 5.3g; Cholesterol 26mg; Calcium 332mg; Fibre 1.7g; Sodium 156mg.

Summer Berry Medley with Red Sauce

Make the most of seasonal fruits in this refreshing, easy-to-make dessert.

Serves 4–6
450–675g/1–1½ lb/4½ cups
    fresh mixed soft summer fruits
    such as strawberries,
    raspberries, blueberries,
    redcurrants and blackcurrants
vanilla ice cream or crème
    fraîche, to serve

For the sauce
175g/6oz/1½ cups redcurrants,
    stripped from their stalks
175g/6oz/1 cup raspberries
50g/2oz/¼ cup caster (superfine)
    sugar
30–45ml/2–3 tbsp crème de
    framboise

1 To make the sauce, place the redcurrants in a bowl with the raspberries, caster sugar and crème de framboise. Cover and leave to macerate for 1–2 hours.

2 Put the macerated fruit, together with its juices, in a pan and cook over a low heat for 5–6 minutes, stirring occasionally, until the fruit is just tender.

3 Pour the fruit into a blender or food processor and process until smooth. Press through a nylon sieve (strainer) to remove any pips (seeds). Leave to cool, then chill.

4 Divide the mixed soft fruit among four individual dishes and pour over the sauce. Serve immediately with vanilla ice cream or crème fraîche.

> **Cook's Tips**
> • The red sauce is also good swirled into mascarpone or plain yogurt. Try it as a topping for peaches or bananas and cream.
> • Crème de framboise is raspberry-flavoured liqueur. You could use Kirsch or an orange-flavoured liqueur instead.

Brown Bread Ice Cream

This delicious textured ice cream is irresistible served with a blackcurrant sauce.

Serves 6
50g/2oz/½ cup roasted and
    chopped hazelnuts, ground
75g/3oz/1½ cups wholemeal
    (whole-wheat) breadcrumbs
50g/2oz/¼ cup demerara (raw)
    sugar
3 egg whites

115g/4oz/generous ⅔ cup caster
    (superfine) sugar
300ml/½ pint/1¼ cups double
    (heavy) cream
a few drops of vanilla extract

For the sauce
225g/8oz/2 cups blackcurrants
75g/3oz/generous ⅓ cup caster
    (superfine) sugar
15ml/1 tbsp crème de cassis
fresh mint sprigs, to decorate

1 Combine the hazelnuts and breadcrumbs on a baking sheet, then sprinkle over the demerara sugar. Place under a medium grill (broiler) and cook until crisp and browned.

2 Whisk the egg whites in a clean, grease-free bowl until stiff, then gradually whisk in the caster sugar until thick and glossy. Whip the cream until soft peaks form and fold into the meringue with the breadcrumb mixture and vanilla extract.

3 Spoon the mixture into a 1.2 litre/2 pint/5 cup loaf tin (pan). Smooth the top level, then cover and freeze until firm.

4 To make the sauce, put the blackcurrants in a small bowl with the sugar. Toss gently to mix and leave for about 30 minutes. Purée the blackcurrants in a food processor or blender, then press through a nylon sieve (strainer) until smooth. Add the crème de cassis and chill.

5 To serve, arrange a slice of ice cream on a plate, spoon over a little sauce and decorate with fresh mint sprigs.

> **Cook's Tip**
> Crème de cassis is the famous French blackcurrant liqueur.

Berry Medley Energy 85kcal/361kJ; Protein 1.3g; Carbohydrate 16.5g, of which sugars 16.5g; Fat 0.2g, of which saturates 0g; Cholesterol 0mg; Calcium 41mg; Fibre 2.6g; Sodium 7mg.
Ice Cream Energy 526kcal/2198kJ; Protein 5.4g; Carbohydrate 55.3g, of which sugars 45.8g; Fat 32.4g, of which saturates 17.1g; Cholesterol 69mg; Calcium 97mg; Fibre 2.2g; Sodium 141mg.

Raspberry Meringue Gâteau

A rich, hazelnut meringue sandwiched with whipped cream and raspberries is the ultimate in elegance.

Serves 6
4 egg whites
225g/8oz/1 cup caster (superfine) sugar
a few drops of vanilla extract
5ml/1 tsp distilled malt vinegar
115g/4oz/1 cup roasted and chopped hazelnuts, ground

300ml/½ pint/1¼ cups double (heavy) cream
350g/12oz/2 cups raspberries
icing (confectioners') sugar, for dusting
fresh mint sprigs, to decorate

For the sauce
225g/8oz/1½ cups raspberries
45–60ml/3–4 tbsp icing (confectioners') sugar, sifted
15ml/1 tbsp orange liqueur

1 Preheat the oven to 180°C/350°F/Gas 4. Grease two 20cm/8in sandwich tins (layer cake pans) and line the bases with baking parchment.

2 Whisk the egg whites in a large clean bowl until they hold stiff peaks, then gradually whisk in the caster sugar a tablespoon at a time, whisking well after each addition. Continue whisking the meringue mixture for a minute of two until very stiff, then fold in the vanilla extract, vinegar and ground hazelnuts.

3 Divide the meringue mixture between the prepared tins and spread level. Bake for 50–60 minutes until crisp. Remove the meringues from the tins and leave them to cool on a wire rack.

4 Meanwhile, make the sauce. Process the raspberries with the icing sugar and liqueur in a blender or food processor, then press through a sieve (strainer) to remove seeds. Chill the sauce.

5 Whip the cream until it forms soft peaks, then gently fold in the raspberries. Sandwich the meringue rounds together with the raspberry cream.

6 Dust the top of the gâteau with icing sugar. Decorate with mint sprigs and serve with the raspberry sauce.

Iced Chocolate & Nut Gâteau

Autumn hazelnuts add crunchiness to this popular iced dinner-party dessert.

Serves 6–8
75g/3oz/¾ cup shelled hazelnuts
about 32 sponge (lady fingers) fingers
150ml/¼ pint/⅔ cup cold strong black coffee

30ml/2 tbsp Cognac or other brandy
450ml/¾ pint/scant 2 cups double (heavy) cream
75g/3oz/⅔ cup icing (confectioners') sugar, sifted
150g/5oz plain (semisweet) chocolate
icing (confectioners') sugar and unsweetened cocoa powder, for dusting

1 Preheat the oven to 200°C/400°F/Gas 6. Spread out the hazelnuts on a baking sheet and toast them in the oven for 5 minutes until golden. Transfer the nuts to a clean dish towel and rub off the skins. Cool, then chop finely.

2 Line a 1.2 litre/2 pint/5 cup loaf tin (pan) with clear film (plastic wrap) and cut the sponge fingers to fit the base and sides. Reserve the remaining fingers.

3 Mix the coffee with the Cognac or other brandy in a shallow dish. Dip the sponge fingers briefly into the coffee mixture and return to the tin, sugary-side down.

4 Whip the cream with the icing sugar until it holds soft peaks. Roughly chop 75g/3oz of the chocolate, and fold into the cream with the hazelnuts.

5 Melt the remaining chocolate in a heatproof bowl set over a pan of barely simmering water. Cool, then fold into the cream mixture. Spoon into the tin.

6 Moisten the remaining sponge fingers in the coffee mixture and lay over the filling. Wrap and freeze until firm.

7 Remove the gâteau from the freezer 30 minutes before serving. Turn out and dust with icing sugar and cocoa powder.

Raspberry Energy 434kcal/1799kJ; Protein 6.8g; Carbohydrate 14.3g, of which sugars 13.9g; Fat 39.3g, of which saturates 17.7g; Cholesterol 69mg; Calcium 81mg; Fibre 3.7g; Sodium 56mg.
Iced Chocolate Energy 631kcal/2628kJ; Protein 8.2g; Carbohydrate 49.7g, of which sugars 38.3g; Fat 44.9g, of which saturates 23.3g; Cholesterol 192mg; Calcium 90mg; Fibre 1.5g; Sodium 57mg.

Cherry Syllabub

This recipe follows the style of the earliest syllabubs from the sixteenth and seventeenth centuries, producing a frothy creamy layer over a liquid one. It's easy to make and delicious.

Serves 4
225g/8oz/2 cups ripe dark cherries, stoned (pitted) and chopped

30ml/2 tbsp Kirsch
2 egg whites
30ml/2 tbsp lemon juice
150ml/¼ pint/⅔ cup sweet white wine
75g/3oz/generous ¼ cup caster (superfine) sugar
300ml/½ pint/1¼ cups double (heavy) cream

1 Divide the chopped cherries among six tall dessert glasses and sprinkle over the Kirsch.

2 Whisk the egg whites in a clean, grease-free bowl until stiff peaks form. Gently fold in the lemon juice, wine and sugar.

3 In a separate bowl (but using the same whisk), lightly beat the cream, then fold into the egg white mixture.

4 Spoon the cream mixture over the cherries, then chill overnight. Serve straight from the refrigerator.

Cook's Tip
Be careful not to overbeat the egg whites otherwise they will separate, which will spoil the consistency of the dessert. Whip the cream until it just forms soft peaks.

Variation
To ring the changes, try using crushed fresh raspberries or chopped ripe peaches instead of the cherries. Ratafia biscuits (almond macaroons) are the perfect accompaniment.

Damask Cream

It is important not to move this elegant dessert while it is setting, or it will separate.

Serves 4
600ml/1 pint/2½ cups milk
40g/1½ oz/3 tbsp caster (superfine) sugar

several drops of triple-strength rose water
10ml/2 tsp vegetable rennet
60ml/4 tbsp double (heavy) cream
sugared rose petals, to decorate (optional)

1 Gently heat the milk and 25g/1oz/2 tbsp of the sugar, stirring, until the sugar has melted and the temperature of the mixture feels neither hot nor cold. Stir rose water to taste into the milk, then remove the pan from the heat and stir in the rennet.

2 Pour the milk into a serving dish and leave undisturbed for 2–3 hours, until set. Stir the remaining sugar into the cream, then carefully spoon over the junket. Decorate with sugared rose petals, if you wish.

Mandarins in Orange-flower Syrup

Mandarins, tangerines, clementines, mineolas: any of these citrus fruits are suitable to use in this refreshing recipe.

Serves 4
11 mandarins
15ml/1 tbsp icing (confectioners') sugar
10ml/2 tsp orange-flower water

1 Pare some rind from one mandarin and cut it into fine shreds for decoration. Squeeze the juice from two mandarins and reserve it. Peel eight further mandarins, removing the white pith. Arrange the whole fruit in a wide dish.

2 Mix the reserved juice with the icing sugar and orange-flower water and pour over the fruit. Cover and chill. Blanch the rind in boiling water for 30 seconds. Drain, cool and sprinkle over the mandarins, with pistachio nuts if you wish.

Syllabub Energy 531kcal/2201kJ; Protein 3.3g; Carbohydrate 29.6g, of which sugars 29.6g; Fat 40.3g, of which saturates 25.1g; Cholesterol 103mg; Calcium 60mg; Fibre 0.5g; Sodium 54mg.
Damask Energy 183kcal/767kJ; Protein 5.4g; Carbohydrate 17.8g, of which sugars 17.8g; Fat 10.6g, of which saturates 6.6g; Cholesterol 29mg; Calcium 193mg; Fibre 0g; Sodium 69mg.
Mandarins Energy 61kcal/261kJ; Protein 1.2g; Carbohydrate 14.8g, of which sugars 14.8g; Fat 0.1g, of which saturates 0g; Cholesterol 0mg; Calcium 41mg; Fibre 1.5g; Sodium 5mg.

Chocolate Blancmange

An old-fashioned dessert that deserves a revival! Serve with thin cream for a touch of luxury.

Serves 4
60ml/4 tbsp cornflour (cornstarch)
600ml/1 pint/2½ cups milk

40g/1½ oz/3 tbsp caster (superfine) sugar
50–115g/2–4oz plain (semi-sweet) chocolate, chopped
vanilla extract, to taste
white and plain (semisweet) chocolate curls, to decorate

1 Rinse a 750ml/1¼ pint/3 cup fluted mould with cold water and leave it upside down to drain. Blend the cornflour to a smooth paste with a little of the milk.

2 Bring the remaining milk to the boil, preferably in a non-stick pan, then pour on to the blended mixture, stirring constantly.

3 Pour all the milk back into the pan and bring slowly to the boil over low heat, stirring constantly until the mixture boils and thickens. Remove the pan from the heat, then add the sugar, chopped chocolate and a few drops of vanilla extract. Stir until the chocolate has melted.

4 Pour the chocolate mixture into the mould and leave in a cool place for several hours to set.

5 To unmould the blancmange, place a large serving plate on top, then, holding the plate and mould firmly together, invert them. Give both plate and mould a gentle but firm shake to loosen the blancmange, then lift off the mould. Scatter white and plain chocolate curls over the top of the blancmange to decorate, and serve at once.

> **Cook's Tip**
> For a special dinner party, flavour the chocolate mixture with crème de menthe or orange-flavoured liqueur instead of vanilla, and set the blancmange in individual moulds.

Yogurt Ring with Tropical Fruit

An impressive, light and colourful dessert with a truly tropical flavour, combining a magical mix of exotic fruits.

Serves 6
175ml/6fl oz/¾ cup tropical fruit juice
15ml/1 tbsp powdered vegetarian gelatine

3 egg whites
150ml/¼ pint/⅔ cup low-fat natural (plain) yogurt
finely grated rind of 1 lime

For the filling
1 mango
2 kiwi fruit
10–12 physalis (Cape gooseberries), plus extra to decorate
juice of 1 lime

1 Pour the tropical fruit juice into a small pan and sprinkle the powdered gelatine over the surface. Heat gently until the gelatine has dissolved.

2 Whisk the egg whites in a clean, grease-free bowl until they hold soft peaks. Continue whisking hard, gradually adding the yogurt and lime rind.

3 Continue whisking hard and pour in the hot gelatine mixture in a steady stream, until evenly mixed.

4 Quickly pour the mixture into a 1.5 litre/2½ pint/6¼ cup ring mould. Chill the mould until the mixture has set. The mixture will separate into two layers.

5 To make the filling, halve, stone (pit), peel and dice the mango. Peel and slice the kiwi fruit. Remove the husks from the physalis and cut the fruit in half. Toss all the fruits together in a bowl and stir in the lime juice.

6 Run a knife around the edge of the ring to loosen the mixture. Dip the mould quickly into hot water, then place a serving plate on top. Holding the plate and mould firmly together, invert them, then lift off the mould. Spoon all the prepared fruit into the centre of the ring, decorate with extra physalis and serve immediately.

Blancmange Energy 225kcal/954kJ; Protein 5.9g; Carbohydrate 39.2g, of which sugars 25.3g; Fat 6.2g, of which saturates 3.7g; Cholesterol 10mg; Calcium 192mg; Fibre 0.3g; Sodium 74mg.
Yogurt Ring Energy 63kcal/267kJ; Protein 5.4g; Carbohydrate 10.1g, of which sugars 10g; Fat 0.4g, of which saturates 0.2g; Cholesterol 0mg; Calcium 59mg; Fibre 1.1g; Sodium 55mg.

Spiced Pears in Cider

A cider sauce, delicately flavoured with cinnamon and lemon, transforms pears into an elegant dessert.

Serves 4
4 medium-firm pears
250ml/8fl oz/1 cup dry cider

thinly pared strip of lemon rind
1 cinnamon stick
25g/1oz/2 tbsp light muscovado
  (brown) sugar
5ml/1 tsp arrowroot
blanched shreds of lemon rind,
  to decorate

1 Peel the pears thinly, leaving them whole with the stalks on. Place in a pan with the cider, lemon rind and cinnamon. Cover and simmer gently, turning the pears occasionally, for 15–20 minutes, or until tender.

2 Lift out the pears with a slotted spoon. Boil the syrup, uncovered, to reduce by about half. Remove the lemon rind and cinnamon stick, then stir in the sugar.

3 Mix the arrowroot with 15ml/1 tbsp cold water in a small bowl until smooth, then stir into the syrup. Bring to the boil and stir over medium heat until thickened and clear.

4 Pour the sauce over the pears and sprinkle with lemon rind shreds. Leave to cool slightly, before serving.

Cook's Tips
• Any variety of pear can be used for cooking, but choose a firm variety such as Conference for this recipe.
• Using whole pears looks impressive but if you prefer they can be halved and cored before cooking. This will shorten the cooking time slightly.

Variation
The cider can be substituted with red wine for pink-tinted pears.

Fruity Bread Pudding

A delicious old-fashioned family favourite with a lighter, healthier touch for today. The perfect way to round off a family meal.

Serves 4
75g/3oz/2/3 cup mixed dried fruit
150ml/1/4 pint/2/3 cup apple juice

115g/4oz stale brown or white
  bread, diced
5ml/1 tsp mixed (apple pie) spice
1 large banana, sliced
150ml/1/4 pint/2/3 cup skimmed
  milk
15g/1/2 oz/1 tbsp demerara (raw)
  sugar
natural (plain) yogurt, to serve

1 Preheat the oven to 200°C/400°F/Gas 6. Place the mixed dried fruit in a small pan with the apple juice and bring to the boil over medium heat.

2 Remove the pan from the heat and stir in the diced bread, mixed spice and banana. Spoon the mixture into a shallow 1.2 litre/2 pint/5 cup ovenproof dish, then pour over the milk.

3 Sprinkle with demerara sugar and bake for about 25–30 minutes, until the pudding is firm and golden brown. Serve immediately with natural yogurt.

Cook's Tips
• Different types of bread will absorb varying amounts of liquid, so you may need to reduce the amount of milk used to allow for this.
• This is a good way to use up stale, leftover bread. Any type of bread is suitable, but wholemeal (whole-wheat) gives a healthier slant to the dish. Remove the crusts before cutting into dice.

Variation
You can experiment as much as you like with the dried fruit. A mix of raisins, sultanas (golden raisins) and chopped ready-to-eat apricots or dates works well.

Pears Energy 107kcal/454kJ; Protein 0.5g; Carbohydrate 23.2g, of which sugars 23.2g; Fat 0.2g, of which saturates 0g; Cholesterol 0mg; Calcium 25mg; Fibre 3.3g; Sodium 9mg.
Pudding Energy 178kcal/759kJ; Protein 4.4g; Carbohydrate 40.9g, of which sugars 27g; Fat 0.8g, of which saturates 0.1g; Cholesterol 1mg; Calcium 97mg; Fibre 1.1g; Sodium 176mg.

Apple Couscous Pudding

Couscous makes a delicious and healthy family pudding.

Serves 4
600ml/1 pint/2½ cups apple juice
115g/4oz/⅔ cup couscous
40g/1½ oz/scant ¼ cup sultanas (golden raisins)
2.5ml/½ tsp mixed spice
1 large cooking apple, peeled, cored and sliced
25g/1oz/2 tbsp light brown sugar

1 Preheat the oven to 200°C/400°F/Gas 6. Place the apple juice, couscous, sultanas and spice in a pan and bring to the boil, stirring. Cover. Simmer for 10–12 minutes to absorb the liquid.

2 Spoon half the mixture into a 1.2 litre/1 pint/5 cup ovenproof dish and top with half the apple slices. Top with the remaining couscous. Arrange the remaining apple slices overlapping on the top and sprinkle with the sugar. Bake for 25–30 minutes, or until the apples are golden brown. Serve immediately.

Crunchy Gooseberry Crumble

Gooseberries make the perfect filling for this extra special crumble.

Serves 4
500g/1¼ lb/4¼ cups gooseberries
50g/2oz/¼ cup caster (superfine) sugar
75g/3oz/1 cup rolled oats
75g/3oz/1 cup wholemeal (whole-wheat) flour
60ml/4 tbsp sunflower oil
50g/2oz/¼ cup demerara (raw) sugar
30ml/2 tbsp chopped walnuts
natural (plain) yogurt, to serve

1 Preheat the oven to 200°C/400°F/Gas 6. Place the gooseberries in a pan with the caster sugar. Cover the pan and cook over low heat for 10 minutes, until the gooseberries are just tender. Transfer to an ovenproof dish.

2 To make the crumble, place the oats, flour and oil in a bowl and stir with a fork until evenly mixed. Stir in the demerara sugar and walnuts, then spread evenly over the gooseberries. Bake for 25–30 minutes, or until golden. Serve with yogurt.

Gingerbread Upside-down Pudding

A proper pudding goes down well on a cold winter's day. This one is quite quick to make and looks very impressive.

Serves 4–6
sunflower oil, for brushing
15g/½ oz/1 tbsp light soft brown sugar
4 peaches, halved and stoned (pitted), or canned peach halves, drained
8 walnut halves

For the base
130g/4½ oz/1 cup wholemeal (whole-wheat) flour
2.5ml/½ tsp bicarbonate of soda (baking soda)
7.5ml/1½ tsp ground ginger
5ml/1 tsp ground cinnamon
115g/4oz/½ cup muscovado (molasses) sugar
1 egg
120ml/4fl oz/½ cup skimmed milk
50ml/2fl oz/¼ cup sunflower oil

1 Preheat the oven to 180°C/350°F/Gas 4. Brush the base and sides of a 23cm/9in round springform cake tin (pan) with oil. Sprinkle the soft brown sugar evenly over the base.

2 Arrange the peaches, cut-side down, in the tin with a walnut half in each.

3 To make the base, sift together the flour, bicarbonate of soda, ginger and cinnamon, then stir in the sugar. Beat together the egg, milk and oil, then mix into the dry ingredients until smooth.

4 Pour the mixture evenly over the peaches and bake for 35–40 minutes, until firm to the touch. Turn out on to a serving plate. Serve hot with yogurt or custard, if you like.

Cook's Tips
• To turn out the pudding successfully, run the point of a sharp knife round the edge of the pudding, then place a serving plate upside-down on top. Holding the plate and tin together firmly, invert. Release the sides and remove the tin.
• The soft brown sugar caramelizes during baking, creating a delightfully sticky topping.

Couscous Energy 180kcal/767kJ; Protein 2.2g; Carbohydrate 44.6g, of which sugars 29.8g; Fat 0.5g, of which saturates 0g; Cholesterol 0mg; Calcium 26mg; Fibre 0.5g; Sodium 6mg.
Crumble Energy 591kcal/2496kJ; Protein 18.1g; Carbohydrate 84.5g, of which sugars 60.7g; Fat 22.8g, of which saturates 2.1g; Cholesterol 0mg; Calcium 352mg; Fibre 30.3g; Sodium 27mg.
Gingerbread Energy 274kcal/1155kJ; Protein 6.6g; Carbohydrate 42.7g, of which sugars 29.3g; Fat 9.8g, of which saturates 1.1g; Cholesterol 32mg; Calcium 62mg; Fibre 3.3g; Sodium 24mg.

Orange Rice Pudding

In Spain, Greece, Italy and Morocco creamy rice puddings are a favourite dish, especially when sweetened with honey. This version is enhanced with a fresh orange flavour.

Serves 4
50g/2oz/¼ cup short grain
   pudding rice
600ml/1 pint/2½ cups milk

30–45ml/2–3 tbsp clear honey,
   to taste
finely grated rind of ½ small
   orange
150ml/¼ pint/⅔ cup double
   (heavy) cream
15ml/1 tbsp chopped pistachios,
   toasted

1 Mix the rice with the milk, honey and orange rind in a pan and bring to the boil, then reduce the heat, cover the pan with a tight-fitting lid and simmer very gently for about 1¼ hours, stirring regularly.

2 Remove the lid and continue cooking and stirring for about 15–20 minutes, until the rice is creamy.

3 Pour in the cream and simmer for 5–8 minutes longer. Serve the rice sprinkled with the chopped toasted pistachios in individual warmed bowls.

Cook's Tip
Make sure you use short grain rice for this recipe; the small chalky grains absorb liquid well, producing a creamy texture.

Variation
For a more fragrant version, omit the grated orange rind and stir in 15ml/1 tbsp orange flower water, 15ml/1 tbsp ground almonds and 5ml/1 tsp almond extract at step 3, along with the cream. Serve sprinkled with chopped dates and pistachios.

Apple & Blackberry Nut Crumble

This much-loved dish of apples and blackberries is topped with a golden, sweet crumble. The addition of nuts gives an extra-delicious crunchy texture.

Serves 4
900g/2lb (about 4 medium)
   cooking apples, peeled, cored
   and sliced
115g/4oz/½ cup butter, diced,
   plus extra for greasing

115g/4oz/½ cup soft light brown
   sugar
175g/6oz/1½ cups blackberries
75g/3oz/¾ cup wholemeal
   (whole-wheat) flour
75g/3oz/¾ cup plain
   (all-purpose) flour
2.5ml/½ tsp ground cinnamon
45ml/3 tbsp chopped mixed nuts,
   toasted
custard, cream or ice cream,
   to serve

1 Preheat the oven to 180°C/350°F/Gas 4. Lightly butter a 1.2 litre/2 pint/5 cup ovenproof dish.

2 Place the apples in a pan with 25g/1oz/2 tbsp of the butter, 25g/1oz/2 tbsp of the sugar and 15ml/1 tbsp water. Cover with a tight-fitting lid and cook gently for about 10 minutes, until the apples are just tender but still holding their shape.

3 Remove from the heat and gently stir in the blackberries. Spoon the mixture into the ovenproof dish and set aside while you make the topping.

4 To make the crumble topping, sift the flours and cinnamon into a bowl, tipping in any of the bran left in the sieve (strainer). Add the remaining 75g/3oz/6 tbsp butter and rub into the flour with your fingertips until the mixture resembles fine breadcrumbs. Alternatively, you can use a food processor to do this stage for you.

5 Stir in the remaining sugar and the nuts and mix well. Sprinkle the crumble topping over the fruit.

6 Bake the crumble for 35–40 minutes until the top is golden brown. Serve immediately with custard, cream or ice cream.

Pudding Energy 355kcal/1477kJ; Protein 7.4g; Carbohydrate 26.6g, of which sugars 16.5g; Fat 24.8g, of which saturates 14.4g; Cholesterol 60mg; Calcium 206mg; Fibre 0.2g; Sodium 94mg.
Crumble Energy 573kcal/2398kJ; Protein 6.8g; Carbohydrate 68.3g, of which sugars 42.3g; Fat 32.2g, of which saturates 15.7g; Cholesterol 61mg; Calcium 86mg; Fibre 5.6g; Sodium 181mg.

Apple Strudel

This great Austrian dessert is traditionally made with strudel pastry, but it is just as good prepared with ready-made filo pastry.

Serves 4–6

75g/3oz/³⁄₄ cup hazelnuts, chopped and roasted
30ml/2 tbsp nibbed almonds, roasted
50g/2oz/4 tbsp demerara (raw) sugar
2.5ml/¹⁄₂ tsp ground cinnamon
grated rind and juice of ¹⁄₂ lemon
2 large cooking apples, peeled, cored and chopped
50g/2oz/¹⁄₃ cup sultanas (golden raisins)
4 large sheets filo pastry
50g/2oz/4 tbsp unsalted (sweet) butter, melted
sifted icing (confectioners') sugar, for dusting
cream, custard or yogurt, to serve

1 Preheat the oven to 190°C/375°F/Gas 5. In a bowl mix together the hazelnuts, almonds, sugar, cinnamon, lemon rind and juice, apples and sultanas. Set aside.

2 Lay one sheet of filo pastry on a clean dish towel and brush with melted butter. Lay a second sheet on top and brush again with melted butter. Repeat with the remaining two sheets.

3 Spread the fruit and nut mixture over the pastry, leaving a 7.5cm/3in border at each of the shorter ends. Fold the pastry ends in over the filling. Roll up from one long edge to the other, using the dish towel to help.

4 Carefully transfer the strudel to a greased baking sheet, placing it seam-side down. Brush all over with butter and bake for 30–35 minutes until golden and crisp. Dust the strudel generously with icing sugar and serve while still hot with cream, custard or yogurt.

Cook's Tip
Chilled filo pastry sheets are available from most supermarkets. Work quickly with the thin sheets as they dry out rapidly.

Banana, Maple & Lime Crêpes

Crêpes are a treat any day of the week, and they can be made in advance and stored in the freezer for convenience.

Serves 4

115g/4oz/1 cup plain (all-purpose) flour
1 egg white
250ml/8fl oz/1 cup skimmed milk
sunflower oil, for frying

For the filling
4 bananas, sliced
45ml/3 tbsp maple or golden (light corn) syrup
30ml/2 tbsp freshly squeezed lime juice
strips of lime rind, to decorate

1 Beat together the flour, egg white, milk and 50ml/2f oz/¹⁄₄ cup water until the mixture is smooth and bubbly. Chill in the refrigerator until ready to use.

2 Heat a small amount of oil in a non-stick frying pan and pour in enough batter just to coat the base. Swirl it around the pan to coat evenly.

3 Cook until golden, then toss or turn and cook the other side. Place on a plate, cover with foil and keep hot while making the remaining pancakes.

4 To make the filling, place the bananas, syrup and lime juice in a pan and simmer gently for 1 minute. Spoon into the pancakes and fold into quarters. Sprinkle with shreds of lime rind to decorate. Serve immediately.

Cook's Tip
To freeze the crêpes, interleaf them with baking parchment and seal in a plastic bag. They should be used within 3 months.

Variation
Use strawberries instead of bananas, and orange in place of lime.

Strudel Energy 298kcal/1247kJ; Protein 4.8g; Carbohydrate 31.6g, of which sugars 18.5g; Fat 17.9g, of which saturates 5.2g; Cholesterol 18mg; Calcium 66mg; Fibre 2.4g; Sodium 55mg.
Crêpes Energy 299kcal/1263kJ; Protein 6.8g; Carbohydrate 57.2g, of which sugars 33g; Fat 6.4g, of which saturates 0.9g; Cholesterol 2mg; Calcium 125mg; Fibre 2g; Sodium 75mg.

Warm Autumn Compôte

This is a simple yet sophisticated dessert featuring succulent ripe autumnal fruits. Serve with vanilla-flavoured cream and thin, crisp cookies.

Serves 4
75g/3oz/generous ¼ cup caster (superfine) sugar
1 bottle red wine
1 vanilla pod (bean), split
1 strip pared lemon rind
4 pears
2 purple figs, quartered
225g/8oz/2 cups raspberries
lemon juice, to taste

1 Put the caster sugar and red wine in a large pan and heat gently until the sugar has completely dissolved. Add the vanilla pod and lemon rind and bring to the boil. Reduce the heat and simmer for 5 minutes.

2 Peel and halve the pears, then scoop out the cores, using a melon baller or teaspoon. Add the pears to the syrup and poach for about 15 minutes, turning them several times so they colour evenly.

3 Add the quartered figs and poach for a further 5 minutes, until the fruits are tender.

4 Transfer the poached pears and figs to a serving bowl using a slotted spoon, then scatter over the raspberries.

5 Return the syrup to the heat and boil rapidly to reduce slightly and concentrate the flavour. Add a little lemon juice to taste. Strain the syrup over the fruits and serve warm.

> **Cook's Tip**
> *Serve with vanilla cream: using 300ml/½ pint/1¼ cups double (heavy) cream, place half in a pan with a vanilla pod (bean). Bring almost to the boil, then cool for 30 minutes. Remove the pod, mix with the remaining cream and add sugar to taste.*

Apple Soufflé Omelette

Apples sautéed until they are slightly caramelized make a delicious autumn filling for this sweet, light-as-air omelette.

Serves 2
4 eggs, separated
30ml/2 tbsp single (light) cream
15g/½oz/1 tbsp caster (superfine) sugar

15g/½ oz/1 tbsp butter
sifted icing (confectioners') sugar, for dredging

For the filling
1 eating apple, peeled, cored and sliced
25g/1oz/2 tbsp butter
25g/1oz/2 tbsp soft light brown sugar
45ml/3 tbsp single (light) cream

1 To make the filling, sauté the apple slices in the butter and sugar until just tender. Stir in the cream and keep warm, while making the omelette.

2 Place the egg yolks in a bowl with the cream and sugar and beat well. Whisk the egg whites until stiff peaks form, then fold into the yolk mixture.

3 Melt the butter in a large heavy frying pan, then pour in the soufflé mixture and spread evenly. Cook for 1 minute until golden underneath, then place under a hot grill (broiler) to brown the top.

4 Slide the omelette on to a plate, spoon the apple mixture on to one side, then fold over. Dredge the icing sugar over thickly, then quickly mark in a criss-cross pattern with a hot metal skewer. Serve immediately.

> **Cook's Tips**
> • *When cooking the top, remove the omelette as soon as it is browned. Do not overcook at this stage otherwise the light texture of the omelette will be damaged.*
> • *You can replace the apples with fresh raspberries or strawberries when they are in season.*

Compôte Energy 318kcal/1342kJ; Protein 2g; Carbohydrate 47.9g, of which sugars 47.9g; Fat 0.5g, of which saturates 0.1g; Cholesterol 0mg; Calcium 84mg; Fibre 6.6g; Sodium 28mg.
Omelette Energy 459kcal/1910kJ; Protein 14.1g; Carbohydrate 24.9g, of which sugars 24.9g; Fat 34.8g, of which saturates 18.1g; Cholesterol 444mg; Calcium 106mg; Fibre 0.6g; Sodium 274mg.

Warm Lemon & Syrup Cake

This simple cake is made special by the lemony syrup which is poured over it when baked.

Serves 8

3 eggs
175g/6oz/³/₄ cup butter, softened
175g/6oz/scant 1 cup caster (superfine) sugar
175g/6oz/1½ cups self-raising (self-rising) flour
50g/2oz/½ cup ground almonds

1.5ml/¼ tsp freshly grated nutmeg
50g/2oz candied lemon peel, finely chopped
grated rind of 1 lemon
30ml/2 tbsp freshly squeezed lemon juice
lemon rind strips, to decorate

For the syrup
175g/6oz/scant 1 cup caster (superfine) sugar
juice of 3 lemons

1 Preheat the oven to 180°C/350°F/Gas 4. Lightly grease and base-line a deep round 20cm/8in cake tin (pan).

2 Place all the cake ingredients in a large bowl and beat well for 2–3 minutes until light and fluffy.

3 Turn the mixture into the prepared tin, spread level and bake for 1 hour, or until golden and firm to the touch.

4 To make the syrup, put the caster sugar, lemon juice and 75ml/5 tbsp water in a pan. Place over low heat and stir until the sugar has completely dissolved, then boil, without stirring, for 1–2 minutes.

5 Turn out the cake on to a plate with a rim. Prick the surface of the cake all over with a fork, then pour over the hot syrup. Leave to soak for about 30 minutes. Cut into slices, and serve the slices warm with lemon strips on top.

> **Cook's Tip**
> To speed up the preparation, mix the ingredients together in a food processor, but take care not to overbeat.

Papaya & Pineapple Crumble

Fruit crumbles are always popular with children and adults, but you can ring the changes with this great exotic variation.

Serves 4–6

175g/6oz/1½ cups plain (all-purpose) flour
75g/3oz/6 tbsp butter, diced
75g/3oz/generous ¼ cup caster (superfine) sugar
75g/3oz/½ cup mixed chopped nuts

For the filling
1 medium-ripe pineapple
1 large ripe papaya
15g/½ oz/1 tbsp caster (superfine) sugar
5ml/1 tsp mixed (apple pie) spice
grated rind of 1 lime
natural (plain) yogurt, to serve

1 Preheat the oven to 180°C/350°F/Gas 4. To make the topping, sift the flour into a bowl and rub in the butter until the mixture resembles breadcrumbs. Stir in the caster sugar and mixed chopped nuts.

2 To make the filling, peel the pineapple, remove the eyes, then cut in half. Cut away the core and cut the flesh into bitesize chunks. Halve the papaya and scoop out the seeds using a spoon. Peel, then cut the flesh into similar size pieces.

3 Put the pineapple and papaya chunks into a large ovenproof dish. Sprinkle over the sugar, mixed spice and lime rind and toss gently to mix.

4 Spoon the crumble topping over the fruit and spread out evenly with a fork, but don't press it down. Bake in the oven for 45–50 minutes, until golden brown. Serve the crumble hot or warm with natural yogurt.

> **Variation**
> If unavailable, the papaya can be replaced with fresh mango.

Syrup Cake Energy 488kcal/2047kJ; Protein 6g; Carbohydrate 66.5g, of which sugars 50.1g; Fat 23.9g, of which saturates 12.3g; Cholesterol 118mg; Calcium 138mg; Fibre 1.4g; Sodium 259mg.
Crumble Energy 403kcal/1690kJ; Protein 5.5g; Carbohydrate 54.8g, of which sugars 32.5g; Fat 19.5g, of which saturates 7.3g; Cholesterol 27mg; Calcium 96mg; Fibre 4g; Sodium 84mg.

Apple & Hazelnut Shortcake

This is a variation on the classic strawberry shortcake and is equally delicious.

Serves 8–10
3 sharp eating apples
5ml/1 tsp lemon juice
15–25g/½–1oz/1–2 tbsp caster (superfine) sugar
15ml/1 tbsp chopped fresh mint, or 5ml/1 tsp dried mint
250ml/8fl oz/1 cup whipping cream
a few drops of vanilla extract

a few fresh mint leaves and whole hazelnuts, to decorate

For the hazelnut shortcake
150g/5oz/1¼ cups plain wholemeal (whole-wheat) flour
50g/2oz/½ cup ground hazelnuts
50g/2oz/½ cup icing (confectioners') sugar, sifted
150g/5oz/generous 1 cup unsalted butter

1 To make the hazelnut shortcake, process the flour, ground hazelnuts and icing sugar with the butter in a food processor in short bursts, until they come together. Bring the dough together, adding a very little iced water if needed. Knead briefly, wrap and chill for 30 minutes.

2 Preheat the oven to 160°C/325°F/Gas 3. Cut the dough in half and roll out each half to an 18cm/7in round. Place on baking parchment on baking sheets. Bake for 40 minutes, or until crisp. Allow to cool.

3 Peel, core and chop the apples into a pan with the lemon juice. Add sugar to taste, then cook for 2–3 minutes, until just soft. Mash the apple gently with the mint and leave to cool.

4 Whip the cream with the vanilla extract. Place one shortbread base on a serving plate. Spread half the apple and half the cream on top.

5 Place the second shortcake on top, then spread over the remaining apple and cream, swirling the top layer of cream gently. Decorate the top with mint leaves and a few whole hazelnuts, then serve at once.

Lemon Cheesecake

A lovely light cream cheese filling is presented on an elegant brandy snap base.

Serves 8
½ x 142g/4¾oz packet lemon jelly (vegetarian gelatine)
45–60ml/3–4 tbsp boiling water
50g/1lb/2 cups low-fat cream cheese

10ml/2 tsp grated lemon rind
75–115g/3–4oz/about ½ cup caster (superfine) sugar
a few drops of vanilla extract
150ml/¼ pint/⅔ cup Greek (US strained plain) yogurt
8 brandy snaps
a few fresh mint leaves and icing sugar, to decorate

1 Dissolve the jelly in the boiling water in a heatproof measuring jug (cup) and, when clear, add enough cold water to make up to 150ml/¼ pint/⅔ cup. Chill until the jelly begins to thicken. Meanwhile, line a 450g/1lb loaf tin (pan) with clear film (plastic wrap).

2 Cream the cheese with the lemon rind, sugar and vanilla and beat until light and smooth. Then fold in the thickening lemon jelly and the yogurt. Spoon into the prepared tin and chill until set. Preheat the oven to 160°C/325°F/Gas 3.

3 Place two or three brandy snaps at a time on a baking sheet. Place in the oven for no more than 1 minute, until soft enough to unroll and flatten out completely. Leave on a cold plate or tray to harden again. Repeat with the remaining brandy snaps.

4 To serve, turn the cheesecake out on to a board with the help of the clear film. Cut into eight slices and place one slice on each brandy snap base. Decorate with mint leaves and dust with icing sugar before serving.

> **Variation**
> Use a packet of orange jelly instead of lemon and use grated orange rind instead of the lemon. Omit the vanilla extract and decorate with pared orange rind shreds in place of mint.

Shortcake Energy 333kcal/1386kJ; Protein 3.3g; Carbohydrate 23.1g, of which sugars 13.8g; Fat 25.9g, of which saturates 14.4g; Cholesterol 58mg; Calcium 36mg; Fibre 2.2g; Sodium 99mg.
Cheesecake Energy 237kcal/1000kJ; Protein 10.9g; Carbohydrate 36.3g, of which sugars 33.9g; Fat 7.2g, of which saturates 3g; Cholesterol 14mg; Calcium 119mg; Fibre 0.1g; Sodium 299mg.

Frozen Strawberry Mousse Cake

Children love this cake because it is pink and pretty, and it is just like an ice cream treat.

Serves 4–6

425g/15oz can strawberries in syrup
15ml/1 tbsp powdered
vegetarian gelatine
6 trifle sponges
45ml/3 tbsp strawberry conserve
200ml/7fl oz/scant 1 cup crème fraîche
200ml/7fl oz/scant 1 cup whipped cream, to decorate

1 Strain the syrup from the strawberries into a large heatproof jug (cup). Sprinkle over the gelatine and stir well. Stand the jug in a pan of hot water and stir until the gelatine has dissolved.

2 Leave to cool, then chill in the refrigerator for just under 1 hour, until beginning to set. Meanwhile, cut the sponge cake in half lengthways, then spread the cut surfaces evenly with the strawberry conserve.

3 Slowly whisk the crème fraîche into the strawberry jelly, then whisk in the canned strawberries. Line a deep 20cm/8in loose-based cake tin (pan) with non-stick baking parchment.

4 Pour half the strawberry mousse mixture into the tin, arrange the sponge cakes over the surface and then spoon over the remaining mousse mixture, pushing down any sponge cakes which rise up.

5 Freeze for 1–2 hours until firm. Unmould the cake and carefully remove the lining paper. Transfer to a serving plate. Decorate with whirls of cream, a few strawberry leaves and a fresh strawberry, if you have them.

> **Cook's Tip**
> *For a glamorous finishing touch, spoon the whipped cream into a piping (pastry) bag fitted with a star nozzle and pipe swirls.*

Frozen Lemon Soufflé with Blackberry Sauce

This tangy iced dessert is complemented wonderfully by the richly coloured blackberry sauce.

Serves 6

grated rind of 1 lemon and juice of 2 lemons
15ml/1 tbsp powdered vegetarian gelatine
5 eggs, separated
150g/5oz/1¼ cups caster (superfine) sugar
a few drops of vanilla extract
400ml/14fl oz/1⅔ cups whipping cream

For the sauce

175g/6oz/1½ cups blackberries (fresh or frozen)
25–40g/1–1½oz/2–3 tbsp caster (superfine) sugar
a few fresh blackberries and blackberry leaves, to decorate

1 Place the lemon juice in a small pan and heat through. Sprinkle on the gelatine and leave to dissolve, or gently heat further until clear. Allow to cool.

2 Put the lemon rind, egg yolks, sugar and vanilla extract into a large bowl and whisk until the mixture is very thick, pale and really creamy.

3 Whisk the egg whites in a clean, grease-free bowl until almost stiff. Whip the cream until stiff.

4 Stir the gelatine mixture into the yolk mixture, then fold in the whipped cream and lastly the egg whites. When lightly but thoroughly blended, turn into a 1.5 litre/2½ pint/6¼ cup soufflé dish and freeze for about 2 hours.

5 To make the sauce, place the blackberries in a pan with the sugar and cook for 4–6 minutes until the juices begin to run and all the sugar has dissolved. Pass through a nylon sieve (strainer) to remove the seeds, then chill until ready to serve.

6 When the soufflé is almost frozen, scoop or spoon out on to individual plates and serve with the blackberry sauce.

Mousse Cake Energy 419kcal/1746kJ; Protein 5.1g; Carbohydrate 36.5g, of which sugars 29.1g; Fat 29.1g, of which saturates 18.1g; Cholesterol 148mg; Calcium 73mg; Fibre 0.8g; Sodium 54mg.
Soufflé Energy 438kcal/1821kJ; Protein 7g; Carbohydrate 33.8g, of which sugars 33.8g; Fat 31.6g, of which saturates 18.1g; Cholesterol 229mg; Calcium 90mg; Fibre 0.9g; Sodium 77mg.